Kindergarten Thinking Skills & Key Concepts

TEACHER'S MANUAL

Thinking Skills & Key Concepts Series
📖 Kindergarten 📖 First Grade 📖 Second Grade

Written by
Howard Black
Sandra Parks

Graphic Design by
Howard Black

© 2015
THE CRITICAL THINKING CO.™
www.CriticalThinking.com
Phone: 800-458-4849 • Fax: 541-756-1758
1991 Sherman Ave., Suite 200 • North Bend • OR 97459
ISBN 978-1-60144-768-5

MIX
Paper from responsible sources
FSC® C011935

Reproduction of This Copyrighted Material
The intellectual material in this product is the copyrighted property of The Critical Thinking Co.™ The individual or entity who initially purchased this product from The Critical Thinking Co.™ or one of its authorized resellers is licensed to reproduce (print or duplicate on paper) up to 35 copies of each page in this product per year for use within one home or one classroom. Our copyright and this limited reproduction permission (user) agreement strictly prohibit the sale of any of the copyrighted material in this product. Any reproduction beyond these expressed limits is strictly prohibited without the written permission of The Critical Thinking Co.™ Please visit http://www.criticalthinking.com/copyright for more information. The Critical Thinking Co.™ retains full intellectual property rights on all its products (eBooks, books, and software).
Printed in the United States of America by McNaughton & Gunn, Inc., Saline, MI (Feb. 2015)

Table of Contents

INTRODUCTION
Thinking Skills and Key Concepts v
Program Design vi
Instructional Methods vi
Description of Chapters... viii
Evaluating Thinking Skills Instruction.. ix
Instructional Recommendations.. xi
Vocabulary and Synonyms xii
Guide to Using the Lesson Plans.. xiii

LESSON PLANS
CHAPTER ONE—DESCRIBING COLORS
Teaching Suggestions... 1
Describing Red.. 1
Describing Orange 2
Describing Yellow.. 3
Describing Green 4
Describing Blue 5
Describing Purple 6
Describing Brown 7
Describing Black 8
Describing White 9
Naming Colors 10
Matching Pictures to Colors 11

CHAPTER TWO—DESCRIBING SHAPES
Teaching Suggestions... 12
Describing Lines.. 13
Describing Circles 14
Finding Circles 15
Drawing Circles 16
Describing Ovals 17
Describing Angles - Lines That Touch 18
Describing Squares... 19
Finding Squares 20
Drawing Squares... 21
Describing Rectangles 21
Finding Rectangles 22
Drawing Rectangles 23
Describing Triangles 24
Finding Triangles... 25
Drawing Triangles 26
Describing Hexagons 26
Drawing Hexagons 27
Tracing Shapes 28

Matching Shapes and Colors	29
Describing Size	31
Describing Solids - Cube and Sphere	32
Describing Solids - Cone and Cylinder	33
Describing Flat or Solid	34
Describing Shapes	35

CHAPTER THREE—SIMILARITIES AND DIFFERENCES IN SHAPES
Teaching Suggestions	37
Matching Shapes	37
Matching by Shape and Color	38
How Alike and Different	39-40

CHAPTER FOUR—SEQUENCES OF SHAPES
Teaching Suggestions	41
What Color Square Comes Next?	41
What Color Squares Come Next?	42
What Comes Next?	43
Describing a Sequence	44

CHAPTER FIVE—KINDS OF SHAPES
Comparing Characteristics	45
Describing a Group - What Belongs?	46
Which Shape Does Not Belong?	47
Sorting Shapes	49

CHAPTER SIX—THINKING ABOUT FAMILY MEMBERS
Teaching Suggestions	50
Describing Family Members	52
Similar Family Members	55

CHAPTER SEVEN—THINKING ABOUT FOOD
Teaching Suggestions	57
Describing Food	59
Describing Parts of a Whole	64
Similar Foods	65
Kinds of Food	68

CHAPTER EIGHT—THINKING ABOUT ANIMALS
Teaching Suggestions	70
Describing Animals	72
Similar Animals	81
Similarities and Differences	85
Kinds of Animals	86

CHAPTER NINE—THINKING ABOUT JOBS
- Teaching Suggestions.. 92
- Describing Jobs... 94
- Similar Jobs... 98
- Similarities and Differences 101
- Kinds of Jobs... 102

CHAPTER TEN—THINKING ABOUT VEHICLES
- Teaching Suggestions.. 106
- Describing Vehicles 107
- Naming Vehicles 109
- Characteristics of Vehicles 110
- Describing Vehicles.. 111
- Describing Parts of a Bicycle 112
- Describing Parts of a Fire Truck 113
- Similar Vehicles.. 114
- Similarities and Differences... 118
- Kinds of Vehicles.. 120
- Match Drivers to their Vehicles 125

CHAPTER ELEVEN—THINKING ABOUT BUILDINGS
- Teaching Suggestions.. 126
- Describing Buildings 128
- Describing Parts of a House 132
- Similar Buildings 133
- Similarities and Differences... 136
- Kinds of Buildings 138

CHAPTER TWELVE—THINKING AND WRITING ABOUT POSITION
- Writing About Position - Above and Below 142
- Writing About Position - Inside and Outside.. 144
- Writing About Position - Front and Behind 145
- Writing About Position - Between and Beside 146

APPENDIX
- Cube Pattern... 148
- Word list - FOOD 149
- Word list - ANIMALS 150
- Word list - JOBS 151
- Word list - VEHICLES 152
- Word list - BUILDINGS 153
- How are two things ALIKE? 154
- Branching Diagram - 2 branches 155
- Branching Diagram - 3 branches 156
- Branching Diagram - 4 branches 157
- Branching Diagram - 5 branches 158

THINKING SKILLS AND KEY CONCEPTS

GOALS/STUDENT OUTCOMES

- Improve young children's vocabulary development and observation skills
- Clarify thinking processes required for content learning (describing, identifying similarities and differences, sequencing, classifying, and recognizing analogies)
- Improve students' understanding of mathematics, social studies and science concepts taught in kindergarten

THINKING SKILLS INSTRUCTION

FIGURAL SKILLS
Describing Shapes
Naming shapes, finding shapes to match a description, and describing characteristics of a shape
Figural Similarities and Differences
Matching shapes
Figural Sequences
Recognizing and producing the next figure in a sequence
Figural Classification
Classifying by shape and/or color, forming classes
Describing Things
Matching a picture to a description, describing people or objects shown in pictures, describing parts of a whole
Verbal Similarities and Differences
Selecting similar family members, occupations, food, animals, vehicles, and buildings, explaining how they are alike or different
Verbal Classifications
Explaining characteristics of a class, exceptions, and sorting objects or people into classes

CONTENT OBJECTIVES

MATHEMATICS OBJECTIVES
Properties of polygons and Solids
Naming polygons and solids, observing sides and angles, expressing the properties of common polygons and solids
Reading and writing mathematical terms
Recognizing and using geometry terms, ordinal numbers, and positional words
Pattern Recognition
Recognizing sequential patterns

SOCIAL STUDIES CONCEPTS
Family members
Age, gender, relationships
Occupations
Consumer/producer, goods/services, community helpers
Buildings
Residences, businesses, government, and storage buildings,
Vehicles
Passenger, public transportation, recreation, and emergency vehicles

SCIENCE CONCEPTS
Food
Plant or animal products, preparation, type of food (dairy, meat, vegetable, grain), part of the plant we eat (root, stem, leaf, fruit)
Animals
Type of animal (fish, bird, mammal, amphibian, reptile), habitat, locomotion, reproduction, skin covering

METHODS TO IMPROVE THINKING AND LEARNING

DIRECT INSTRUCTION
Prior knowledge, clear objectives, practice, metacognition, application

DEVELOPMENTAL FORMS
Concrete (pictures and picture books), semi-concrete (student book), abstract (discussion)

COOPERATIVE LEARNING
Paired problem solving, think/pair/share

GRAPHIC ORGANIZERS
Graphics to show thinking (description, compare/contrast, order, and class relationships)

WHOLE SENTENCE RESPONDING
In both thinking skills activities and in general instruction students and teachers speak and write in whole sentences

MENTAL MODELS
Graphics show key characteristics of mathematics, social studies, and science concepts

LANGUAGE INTEGRATION ACTIVITIES
Developmental activities supplement vocabulary acquisition and include drawing activities, creating big books, story telling, writing, and discussing picture books

PROGRAM EVALUATION

- Student performance on language proficiency and cognitive abilities tests
- Student performance on normed-referenced or criterion-referenced achievement tests
- Improved student writing
- Number of students placed in advanced academic classes, including gifted programs, and subsequent successful performance in such classes

INTRODUCTION

PROGRAM DESIGN

Rationale
Thinking Skills & Key Concepts is a program is designed to:

- Improve young children's observation and description skills
- Develop academic vocabulary
- Clarify thinking processes that underlie content learning (identifying and describing/defining, similarities and differences, sequencing, and classifying)
- Improve students' understanding of important mathematics, social studies and science concepts taught in kindergarten

In *Kindergarten Thinking Skills & Key Concepts* lessons, students describe the properties of geometric shapes, family members, occupations, animals, food, vehicles, or buildings. Students clarify their thinking by peer and class discussion of richly detailed photographs.

Thinking Skills
The thinking skills developed in this program include describing, finding similarities and differences, sequencing, and classifying. These processes were selected because of their prevalence in academic disciplines, particularly mathematics and science instruction. Students must be proficient in these thinking skills because the Common Core State Standards and most state standards emphasize concept development and reading comprehension.

These thinking processes are commonly featured on objective tests. Since improved school performance is an important goal of thinking skills instruction, exercises provide many variations of each thinking skill. Within each chapter thinking skills are sequenced in the order in which a child develops intellectually. A learner first observes and describes objects, recognizes their characteristics, and distinguishes similarities and differences between them. Describing, comparing, and contrasting are necessary to put objects or events in order and to group objects by class.

To transfer thinking skills to other contexts, students must remember the steps in their own thinking. They practice metacognition of the thinking skill in each lesson. In each chapter lessons feature the same thinking processes, giving students many transfer examples. This repetition builds students' confidence and competence as thinkers and learners.

Academic Vocabulary Development
Students discuss detailed photographs in order to discuss key mathematic, science, and social studies terms. Through peer discussion learners with limited vocabulary hear and express the properties of key academic concepts.

Common Core State Standards promote increased use of non-fiction books to improve reading comprehension and background in science and social studies. They also emphasize writing as a technique for improved content learning. *Thinking Skills & Key Concepts* features numerous activities for listening, speaking, and writing to accomplish these goals.

INSTRUCTIONAL METHODS

Direct Instruction
Each chapter features direct instruction for each thinking process. When introducing a skill, the teacher identifies a school-related or nonacademic example in which the learner has used that thinking process, cueing the learner that he or she already has some experience and competence with that skill.

Stating the lesson objective clarifies both the content and the thinking skill.

The Thinking About Thinking section of each lesson reminds students of the thinking process practiced in the lesson. Research on thinking process instruction indicates that, without metacognition, subsequent transfer is less likely. Metacognition is fostered by peer and class discussion. The learner then identifies other contexts in which he or she has used this skill. This association with past personal experience increases the learner's confidence in his or her thinking and encourages transfer of the skill.

Developmental Forms

Colored drawings, photographs, and picture books depict the significant details and illustrate examples of key concepts. Peer and class discussion clarify concepts and promote vocabulary.

Listening and speaking employ different learning styles, allowing students to recognize different ways to describe an object. Discussion reinforces the learner's memory of the thinking process, promotes transfer to similar tasks, and enhances the learner's confidence and willingness to participate in class.

Kindergarten students trace and copy mathematic, science, and social studies terms as they begin to express them in model sentences.

Cooperative Learning

Peer discussion significantly enhances language acquisition, particularly for second-language learners. Through conversations each student hears and expresses both the thinking process and the content. Before students learn to read (an in-put process), they first listen (a more basic in-put process). Before students write (an out-put process), they first speak (a more basic out-put process).

Many students have limited experience listening or speaking for a sustained period. Peer discussion promotes the quality and accuracy of students' responses. Evaluation of thinking skills instruction shows that young children, particularly bilingual students, gain confidence and willingness to participate in class discussion when they have had an opportunity to "rehearse" their comments with a partner.

Whole-Sentence Responding

In *Kindergarten Thinking Skills & Key Concepts* lessons, students and teachers respond in whole sentences. Teachers who have used this technique report that this practice is so significant in promoting students' language proficiency that it should be considered an essential element of instruction.

Mental Models

A mental model is a framework that features the key characteristics that one must know to understand a concept. A mental model helps a learner to:

- Find what one needs to know to understand a new concept
- Remember the characteristics
- State clear definitions or adequate descriptions
- Explain a concept to someone else

By the end of each chapter kindergarten students should know the significant characteristics of each of the concepts listed below. Teachers should use picture books or actual objects, when possible, to illustrate the following key characteristics.

CONCEPT	KEY CHARACTERISTICS
Polygon	Lines (curved or straight), sides (equal or unequal), number of sides, size of angles
Solids	Number of faces, what shape is seen from each side
Patterns	Describing color, size, and shape, color/size/shape sequences
Family	Relationship, age, gender, role in the family

Food (animals)	Color, liquid or solid, how we eat them, taste, how prepared
Food (plants)	Type (vegetable, fruit, grain, seed), part of plant we eat (leaf, root, stem, fruit), kind of plant (vine, bush, tree), taste, color/shape/size, how prepared
Animals	Type (mammals, birds, fish, reptiles), live birth/hatch from eggs, size shape/color, appearance, habitat, how it moves (fast, slow)
Jobs	Types of jobs (provides goods or services, emergency workers, health care workers), equipment, special clothing, building where they work, training
Vehicles	Types of vehicles (emergency, personal, work, public transportation, recreation), size, number of passengers, where it travels (land/sea/air), speed
Buildings	Types of buildings (residences, government buildings, businesses, storage), size, number of people who live there, what is sold or stored there, special features

Language Integration Activities

Language acquisition research suggests several strategies to help young children develop and express new or partially conceived concepts. *Kindergarten Thinking Skills & Key Concepts* lesson plans include drawing activities, portfolio assessment, creating big books, storytelling, and writing exercises.

- **Drawing activities:** Students illustrate details of concepts explored in the *Kindergarten Thinking Skills & Key Concepts* program (family members, jobs, food, vehicles, animals, and buildings).

- **Creating "big books":** Drawings are collected to form individual or class "big books" to show students' understanding and growth.

- **Storytelling:** Personal narratives and imaginative stories extend concept development in the *Kindergarten Thinking Skills & Key Concepts* program.

- **Writing:** Students create sentences, definitions, paragraphs, and full stories about concepts featured in the *Kindergarten Thinking Skills & Key Concepts* lessons.

- **Picture Book Extension:** Fiction and nonfiction books for kindergarten students depict and explain important concepts. Common Core State Standards emphasize using non-fiction books to promote reading comprehension and to teach science and social studies objectives. Consult your school librarian to identify appropriate books, particularly picture books that show cultural diversity.

DESCRIPTION OF CHAPTERS

Describing Colors
The exercises in Chapter 1 feature matching various colors to geometric shapes and photographs of common objects. Students learn that color is an important property when describing foods, plants, animals, vehicles, buildings, and geometric figures.

Describing Shapes
Students name shapes, observe the sides and angles, and write about the properties of common geometric figures and three-dimensional objects.

Similarities and Differences - Shapes
Chapter 3 features activities to develop visual discrimination skills. Describing size, shape, and color are basic observations in geometry, life sciences, and earth sciences.

Sequences of Shapes
In Chapter 4 students evaluate and produce a variety of sequences involving color and shape.

Kinds of Shapes
In Figural Classification exercises students identify common characteristics and group geometric figures by class.

Thinking About Family Members
Students describe family members, compare and contrast them, and classify them. They discuss age, gender, relationship to other family members, roles, and interests or experiences that make various family members special.

Thinking About Food
Students describe, compare and contrast, and classify food. They discuss whether food is a plant or animal product, its appearance and taste, and how it is prepared across cultures. To describe food products from plants, students identify the parts of a plant that we eat: root, stem, leaf, fruit, and/or seed.

Thinking About Animals
Students learn types of animals (fish, birds, reptiles, mammals), and describe, compare, contrast, and classify them. They discuss whether various animals are cold-blooded or warm-blooded, give live birth or eggs, have a backbone, appearance (color, size, body covering), where it lives, and how it moves.

Thinking About Occupations
Students describe, compare and contrast, and classify occupations. They discuss whether jobs provide goods or services, how much training is required, the activities of various professions, and the equipment and uniforms associated with the profession. They learn types of jobs: producers, health workers, government workers, and service providers.

Thinking About Vehicles
Students describe, compare and contrast, and classify vehicles. They discuss the size and purpose of various vehicles, where they are driven, their appearance, ownership, and the kind of equipment they contain.

Thinking About Buildings
Students describe, compare and contrast, and classify buildings. They discuss the size, purpose, construction, design, materials, and location of various buildings, as well as who lives or works there, and who owns it.

EVALUATING THINKING SKILLS INSTRUCTION

Thinking skills instruction has been evaluated using many assessment procedures:
- Student performance on cognitive abilities tests
- Student performance on normed-referenced achievement tests
- Student performance on criterion-referenced achievement tests
- Student performance on language proficiency tests
- Number of students placed in heterogeneous grouped classes, or advanced academic programs, as well as students' subsequent successful performance in gifted or academic excellence classes

Cognitive Abilities Tests

The figural and verbal subtests of cognitive abilities tests are closely correlated to the goals and activities in *Kindergarten Thinking Skills & Key Concepts.*

The following cognitive abilities tests have been used in program effectiveness evaluation of thinking instruction using the *Kindergarten Thinking Skills & Key Concepts* series:

- Cognitive Abilities Test (Woodcock-Johnson)
  Riverside Publishing Company
  425 Spring Lake Dr.
  Itasa, IL 60143
  800-323-9540 • 312-693-0325 (fax)

- Developing Cognitive Abilities Test
  American College Testronics
  (formerly American Testronics)
  P.O. Box 2270
  Iowa City, IA 52244
  800-533-0030 • 319-337-1578 (fax)

- Test of Cognitive Skills
  CTB-McGraw Hill
  P.O. Box 150
  Monterey, CA 93942-0150
  800-538-9547 • 800-282-0266 (fax)

Norm-Referenced Achievement Tests

Composite scores on norm-referenced achievement tests are generally poor indicators of improved thinking skills. Some subtests do reflect the thinking skills addressed in *Kindergarten Thinking Skills & Key Concepts* instruction. Program evaluation using this series has indicated substantial gains in subtests which measure reading comprehension and mathematics concepts. If achievement test information is used to report the effectiveness of *Kindergarten Thinking Skills & Key Concepts* instruction, only those subtests should be reported.

Language Proficiency Tests

Program evaluation of *Kindergarten Thinking Skills & Key Concepts* shows substantial gains in vocabulary, reading comprehension, and mathematics. Anecdotal data, and students' drawings show unusual conceptualization of primary science and social studies concepts. Students using *Thinking Skills & Key Concepts* are found to be well prepared for first and second grade instruction in science and social studies commonly measured by state and local assessments. Because one goal of the *Kindergarten Thinking Skills & Key Concepts* program is language development, increased vocabulary can be shown on a variety of language tests. Tests commonly used to evaluate the effect of thinking instruction on language development include the following:

- Peabody Picture Vocabulary Test
- ESOL proficiency tests

Inclusion and Performance in Mainstream or Advanced Academic Programs

The *Thinking Skills & Key Concepts* series is commonly used to promote access to academic excellence programs or to prepare students to be successful in mainstream classes from special services programs (Chapter 1 classes, bilingual programs, ESOL classes, special education classes, or remedial programs). This goal is evaluated by the number of students who gain access to programs, the speed with which the transition is accomplished, and the students' level of achievement when placed in general or advanced classes.

INSTRUCTIONAL RECOMMENDATIONS

- **Do description and similarities and differences exercises first.** These two processes are required for sequencing and classifying.

- **Encourage peer discussion.** The quality of student responses and their attentiveness significantly improve when peers discuss their answers before class discussion. Peer discussion is particularly effective in special education, bilingual, and Title I classes.

- **Conduct short exercises.** Each page usually takes one 20-30 minute session in order to have time for the "Thinking About Thinking" and "Personal Application" activities. Discuss a few exercises with ample time for students to explain their thinking, rather than conducting additional lessons.

- **Identify and use students' background knowledge.** Use these lessons to diagnose students' prior knowledge. Remember the language that students use in their descriptions. Use the same words to remind students of the thinking processes in subsequent social studies and science lessons.

- **Use *Thinking Skills & Key Concepts* lessons before or after social studies or science activities.** Possible responses in each lesson plan exceed the answers commonly expected from students in kindergarten. Continue accepting students comments until key characteristics have been mentioned.

- **Teach other mathematics, science, and social studies concepts using the same thinking processes.** Use correct terms for the thinking process to cue students to transfer the thinking process to other contexts. Use the same methods (peer and class discussion, observation of pictures or objects, etc.) in other lessons.

- **Insist that students use complete sentences when responding.** Students whose language proficiency is underdeveloped are inclined to answer in single words or phrases. To realize the language acquisition benefits of these lessons, students should answer in complete sentences, expressing whole thoughts that are grammatically correct.

- **Lessons should not be given as homework assignments or as independent activities.** The lessons in *Thinking Skills & Key Concepts* are designed to enhance cognitive development through discussion and observation. Exercises from the student book should not be used as a substitute for class discussion.

VOCABULARY AND SYNONYMS

Reinforce the language of thinking in thinking skills activities and in other lessons. The following list includes terms that teachers and students use in *Thinking Skills & Key Concepts* lessons. Students may create a "thinking thesaurus" of the words and idioms that they use to describe their thinking. Encourage them to express their thinking using the terms below.

WORD	SYNONYMS
Arrange	place, assemble, organize, put together, gather, build,
Category	class, group, kind, type
Class	group, category, kind, type
Classify	arrange, group
Compare	match, find similarities
Contrast	unlike, find differences
Decrease	lessen, shrink, become smaller
Definition	meaning, explanation, description
Describe	explain, give details
Detail	part, piece
Difference	unlike, contrasts, not like
Discuss	talk about, describe, explain
Eliminate	remove, take out, erase, end
Equal	same, matching, same size
Examine	find the details, look at
Explain	make sure, show, tell
False	not true, not real, untrue, unreal
Figural	drawn, geometric
Figure	shape, diagram, drawing
Geometric	figural, having shape
Identify	find, recognize, pick out, show
Locate	identify, place, find
Location	place, position
Matching	equal, making an equal pair
Member	belongs to a group or class
Observe	pay attention to, examine, look at carefully
Order	rank, sequence
Part	piece, detail
Pattern	arrangement, design
Prepare	produce, create, ready, plan
Produce	make, create, assemble
Recognize	identify, be familiar with
Relationship	connection, how related or similar
Select	pick out, identify, locate, decide
Sequence	steps, order, rank, change
Shape	figure, pattern, drawing
Significant	important, basic
Similarity	likeness, sameness
Sort	group, classify, organize
True	real
Verbal	spoken, said in words
Whole	entire, complete, total

GUIDE TO USING THE LESSON PLANS

LESSON TITLE

CURRICULUM APPLICATIONS: Lists content objectives which feature the skill or require it as a prerequisite.

TEACHING SUGGESTIONS: Alerts the teacher to special vocabulary or concepts in the lesson. Identifies materials or special concerns when conducting the lessons.

LESSON

Introduction: Provides information that the student may not have previously learned or indicates when he or she has used a similar thinking. This step reassures students that they are prepared for the lesson and establishes the pattern of using prior knowledge.

Stating the Objective: Explains to the student what he or she will learn in the lesson. This step previews the directions that the teacher gives when conducting the lesson.

Conducting the Lesson: Provides a sample dialog to emphasize both the content and the thinking process.
    Teacher Comment: **Bold type shows suggested dialogue for teachers.**
    Student Response: Sample student answers.

THINKING ABOUT THINKING: Helps the student clarify and verbalize the thinking process (metacognition).

PERSONAL APPLICATION: Relates the skill to the learner's experience and cues the learner regarding possible future uses of the skill.

Kindergarten Thinking Skills & Key Concepts — Teacher's Manual

CHAPTER ONE – DESCRIBING COLORS (Pages 2-14)

TEACHING ABOUT COLORS

CURRICULUM APPLICATIONS
Language Arts: Reading readiness lessons that involve color; speaking and writing activities suitable for kindergarten students
Mathematics: Describing objects that are examples of geometric shapes
Science: Describing organisms or objects by color
Social Studies: Describing buildings and artifacts of various cultures
Enrichment Areas: Recognizing road signs; following directions in art lessons

LANGUAGE INTEGRATION ACTIVITIES

- As each color is discussed, ask students to cut out pictures of objects that are good examples of the eight colors discussed in this chapter. Organize their pictures into a bulletin board display, labeling the groups by color.

- Integrate these color terms into your language arts program by discussing picture books that emphasize color.

TEACHING SUGGESTIONS

- Students should discuss and explain their answers in complete sentences. When asked the color of a tulip, a student may correctly answer "red." If a student responds, "A tulip is red," he or she has named the flower and its characteristics, stating the type of plant and stating its properties. This practice seems artificial at first, but it is important for young children, especially second-language learners, to hear and speak in complete sentences.

- Show actual objects when possible.

Page 2: DESCRIBING RED

TEACHING SUGGESTIONS
- Identify objects, as well as color. Young children, particularly second-language learners, may not be familiar with these objects, plants, and animals, as well as the terms used to describe them.

LESSON

Introduction
Color is an important attribute used to describe objects.

Stating the Objective
Teacher Comment: **In this lesson you will identify the red object in each row.**

Conducting the Lesson
Teacher Comment: **The first row contains four shapes. The circle looks like an "O." The square has four sides. The triangle has three sides. The shape with six sides is a hexagon. Which shape is red?**
  Student Response: The triangle is red.
Teacher Comment: **Circle the red triangle.**

Teacher Comment: **The second row has four shapes: a rectangle, a square, a triangle, and a circle. The rectangle has four sides but the sides are not all the same length like the square. Which shape is red?**
  Student Response: The square is red.
Teacher Comment: **Circle the red square.**

Teacher Comment: **The third row contains four signs. The first sign tells a driver to stop. The second sign shows that a hospital is nearby. The third sign tells the driver to slow down for a curve in the road. The last sign shows where the parking lot is located. Which sign is red?**

Kindergarten Thinking Skills & Key Concepts   Teacher's Manual

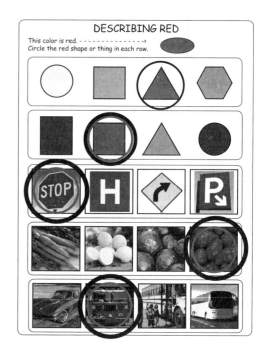

    Student Response: The stop sign is red.
    Teacher Comment: **Circle the red stop sign.**

    Teacher Comment: **The fourth row shows four foods: carrots, lemons, cabbages, and strawberries. Which food is red?**
    Student Response: The strawberries are red.
    Teacher Comment: **Circle the red strawberries.**

    Teacher Comment: **The last row shows four vehicles: a car, a fire truck, a school bus, and a city bus. Which vehicle is red?**
    Student Response: The fire truck is red.
    Teacher Comment: **Circle the red fire truck.**

Thinking About Thinking
    Teacher Comment: **What did you pay attention to in order to find the right color?**
    Student Response:
        1. I paid attention to the color of the example.
        2. I looked for the same color.
        3. I named the shape or object that is the same color.

Personal Application
    Teacher Comment: **When do you have to name a color?**
    Student Response: I name a color to make requests (e.g. "Please hand me that red block, not the blue one.") or to give directions (e.g. "Wait until the light turns green.")

Page 3: DESCRIBING ORANGE

LESSON

Stating the Objective
    Teacher Comment: **In this lesson you will identify the orange object in each row.**

Conducting the Lesson
    Teacher Comment: **What are the shapes in the first row?**
      Student Response: The shapes are a hexagon, a circle, a square, and a triangle.
    Teacher Comment: **Which shape is orange?**
      Student Response: The square is orange.
    Teacher Comment: **Circle the orange square.**

    Teacher Comment: **Name the shapes in the second row.**
      Student Response: The shapes are a rectangle, a triangle, a hexagon, and a circle.
    Teacher Comment: **Which shape is orange?**
      Student Response: The triangle is orange.
    Teacher Comment: **Circle the orange triangle.**

    Teacher Comment: **The third row shows four animals: an ostrich, a shark, a camel, and a goldfish. Which animal is orange?**
      Student Response: The goldfish is orange.
    Teacher Comment: **The fourth row shows fruit: an orange, apples, bananas, and grapes. Which fruit is orange?**
      Student Response: The orange is orange.
    Teacher Comment: **Circle the orange orange.**

Teacher Comment: **The bottom row shows food: pumpkins, lemons, tomatoes, and onions. Which food is orange?**
   Student Response: The pumpkins are orange.
Teacher Comment: **Circle the orange pumpkins.**

Thinking About Thinking
   Teacher Comment: **What did you pay attention to in order to find the right color?**
   Student Response:
      1. I paid attention to the color of the example.
      2. I looked for the same color.
      3. I named the shape or object that is the same color.

Personal Application
   Teacher Comment: **When do you have to name a color?**
   Student Response: I name a color to make requests (e.g. "Please hand me that red block, not the blue one.") or to give directions (e.g. "Wait until the light turns green.")

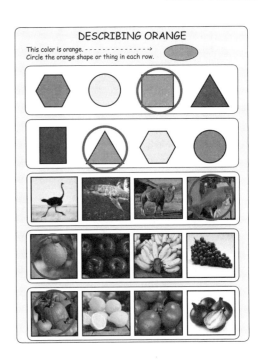

Page 4: DESCRIBING YELLOW

LESSON

Stating the Objective
   Teacher Comment: **In this lesson you will identify the yellow object in each row.**

Conducting the Lesson
   Teacher Comment: **What are the shapes in the first row?**
      Student Response: The shapes are a square, a triangle, a circle, and a hexagon.
   Teacher Comment: **Which shape is yellow?**
      Student Response: The circle is yellow.
   Teacher Comment: **Circle the yellow circle.**

   Teacher Comment: **What are the names of the shapes in the second row?**
      Student Response: The shapes are a circle, a square, a hexagon, and a triangle.
   Teacher Comment: **Which shape is yellow?**
      Student Response: The triangle is yellow.
   Teacher Comment: **Circle the yellow triangle.**

   Teacher Comment: **This third row shows food: butter, bread, bacon and eggs. Which food is yellow?**
      Student Response: The butter is yellow.
   Teacher Comment: **Circle the yellow butter.**

   Teacher Comment: **The fourth row shows vehicles: a school bus, a freight train, an automobile, and a pickup truck. Which vehicle is yellow?**
      Student Response: The school bus is yellow.
   Teacher Comment: **Circle the yellow school bus.**

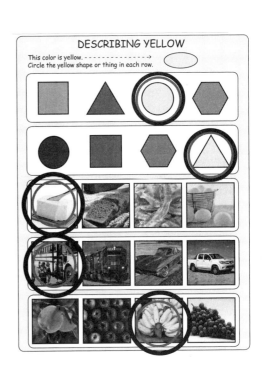

Teacher Comment: **The bottom row shows fruit: peaches, apples, bananas, and grapes. Which fruit is yellow?**
   Student Response: The bananas are yellow.
Teacher Comment: **Circle the yellow bananas.**

Thinking About Thinking
   Teacher Comment: **What did you pay attention to in order to find the right color?**
   Student Response:
   1. I paid attention to the color of the example.
   2. I looked for the same color.
   3. I named the shape or object that is the same color.

Personal Application
   Teacher Comment: **When do you have to name a color?**
   Student Response: I name a color to make requests (e.g. "Please hand me that red block, not the blue one.") or to give directions (e.g. "Wait until the light turns green.")

Page 5: DESCRIBING GREEN

LESSON

Stating the Objective
   Teacher Comment: **In this lesson you will identify the green object in each row.**

Conducting the Lesson
   Teacher Comment: **What are the names of the shapes in the first row?**
      Student Response: The shapes are a triangle, a square, a circle, and a hexagon.
   Teacher Comment: **Which shape is green?**
      Student Response: The square is green.
   Teacher Comment: **Circle the green square.**

   Teacher Comment: **What are the names of the shapes in the second row?**
      Student Response: The shapes are a circle, a hexagon, a rectangle, and a triangle.
   Teacher Comment: **Which of the shapes is green?**
      Student Response: The circle is green.
   Teacher Comment: **Circle the green circle.**

   Teacher Comment: **The third row contains four signs: a stop sign, a hospital sign, a caution sign that tells the driver to slow down because there's a curve ahead, and a sign that shows the location of the parking lot. Which sign is green?**
      Student Response: The hospital sign is green.
   Teacher Comment: **Circle the green hospital sign.**

   Teacher Comment: **The fourth row contains food. Name these foods.**
      Student Response: These foods are pumpkins, corn, tomatoes, and broccoli.
   Teacher Comment: **Which food is green?**
      Student Response: The broccoli is green.
   Teacher Comment: **Circle the green broccoli.**

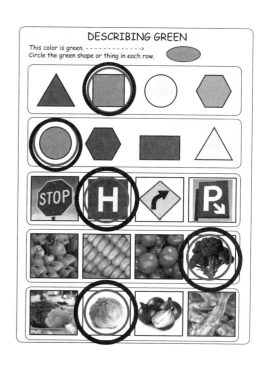

Teacher Comment: **The last row shows a group of food: ham, lettuce, onions, and bacon. Which food is green?**
　　Student Response: The lettuce is green.
　Teacher Comment: **Circle the green lettuce.**

Thinking About Thinking
　Teacher Comment: **What did you pay attention to in order to find the right color?**
　Student Response:
　　1. I paid attention to the color of the example.
　　2. I looked for the same color.
　　3. I named the shape or object that is the same color.

Personal Application
　Teacher Comment: **When do you have to name a color?**
　　Student Response: I name a color to make requests (e.g. "Please hand me that red block, not the blue one.") or to give directions (e.g. "Wait until the light turns green.")

Page 6: DESCRIBING BLUE

LESSON

Stating the Objective
　Teacher Comment: **In this lesson you will identify the blue object in each row.**

Conducting the Lesson
　Teacher Comment: **Name the shapes in the first row.**
　　Student Response: The shapes are a hexagon, a circle, a square, and a triangle.

　Teacher Comment: **Which shape is blue?**
　　Student Response: The square is blue.
　Teacher Comment: **Circle the blue square.**

　Teacher Comment: **Name the shapes in the second row.**
　　Student Response: The shapes are a circle, a rectangle, a square, and a triangle.
　Teacher Comment: **Which shape is blue?**
　　Student Response: The rectangle is blue.
　Teacher Comment: **Circle the blue rectangle.**

　Teacher Comment: **The third row shows four vehicles. Name the vehicles.**
　　Student Response: The vehicles are a bicycle, a pickup truck, a train, and a car.
　Teacher Comment: **Which vehicle is blue?**
　　Student Response: The bicycle is blue.
　Teacher Comment: **Circle the blue bicycle.**

　Teacher Comment: **The fourth row shows four signs: a stop sign, an information sign, a caution sign, and a parking lot sign.**
　Teacher Comment: **Which sign is blue?**
　　Student Response: The parking lot sign is blue.
　Teacher Comment: **Circle the blue parking lot sign.**

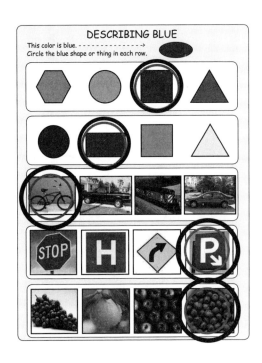

Teacher Comment: **The last row is a group of fruit. Name the fruit.**
   Student Response: The fruits are grapes, an orange, apples, and blueberries.
Teacher Comment: **Which fruit is blue?**
   Student Response: The blueberries are blue.
Teacher Comment: **Circle the blue blueberries.**

Thinking About Thinking
   Teacher Comment: **What did you pay attention to in order to find the right color?**
   Student Response:
      1. I paid attention to the color of the example.
      2. I looked for the same color.
      3. I named the shape or object that is the same color.

Personal Application
   Teacher Comment: **When do you have to name a color?**
   Student Response: I name a color to make requests (e.g. "Please hand me that red block, not the blue one.") or to give directions (e.g. "Wait until the light turns green.")

Page 7: DESCRIBING PURPLE

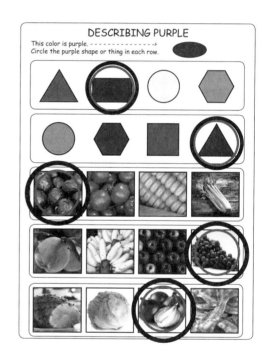

LESSON

Stating the Objective
   Teacher Comment: **In this lesson you will identify the purple object in each row.**

Conducting the Lesson
   Teacher Comment: **Name the shapes in the first row.**
      Student Response: The shapes are a triangle, a rectangle, a circle, and a hexagon.
   Teacher Comment: **Which shape is purple?**
      Student Response: The rectangle is purple.
   Teacher Comment: **Circle the purple rectangle.**

   Teacher Comment: **Name the shapes in the second row.**
      Student Response: The shapes are a circle, a hexagon, a square and a triangle.
   Teacher Comment: **Which shape is purple?**
      Student Response: The triangle is purple.
   Teacher Comment: **Circle the purple triangle.**

   Teacher Comment: **The third row shows a group of vegetables. Name the vegetables.**
      Student Response: The vegetables are cabbages, tomatoes, corn, and celery.
   Teacher Comment: **Which vegetable is purple?**
      Student Response: The cabbages are purple.
   Teacher Comment: **Circle the purple cabbages.**

   Teacher Comment: **The next row shows fruit. Name the fruits.**
      Student Response: The fruits are peaches, bananas, apples, and grapes.
   Teacher Comment: **Which fruit is purple?**
      Student Response: The grapes are purple.
   Teacher Comment: **Circle the purple grapes.**

Kindergarten Thinking Skills & Key Concepts   Teacher's Manual

   Teacher Comment: **Name the foods in the last row.**
     Student Response: The foods are ham, lettuce, onions, and bacon.
   Teacher Comment: **Which food is purple?**
     Student Response: The onions are purple.
   Teacher Comment: **Circle the purple onions.**

Thinking About Thinking
   Teacher Comment: **What did you pay attention to in order to find the right color?**
     Student Response:
      1. I paid attention to the color of the example.
      2. I looked for the same color.
      3. I named the shape or object that is the same color.

Personal Application
   Teacher Comment: **When do you have to name a color?**
     Student Response: I name a color to make requests (e.g. "Please hand me that red block, not the blue one.") or to give directions (e.g. "Wait until the light turns green.")

Page 8: DESCRIBING BROWN

LESSON

Stating the Objective
   Teacher Comment: **In this lesson you will identify the brown object in each row.**

Conducting the Lesson
   Teacher Comment: **Name the shapes in the first row.**
     Student Response: The shapes are a triangle, a rectangle, a circle, and a hexagon.
   Teacher Comment: **Which shape is brown?**
     Student Response: The hexagon is brown.
   Teacher Comment: **Circle the brown hexagon.**

   Teacher Comment: **Name the shapes in the second row.**
     Student Response: The shapes are a square, a hexagon, a triangle, and a circle.
   Teacher Comment: **Which shape is brown?**
     Student Response: The square is brown.
   Teacher Comment: **Circle the brown square.**

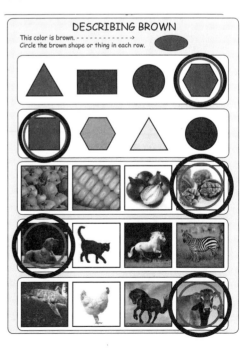

   Teacher Comment: **The third row shows food. Name the foods.**
     Student Response: The foods are pumpkins, corn, onions, and walnuts.
   Teacher Comment: **Which food is brown?**
     Student Response: The walnuts are brown.
   Teacher Comment: **Circle the brown walnuts.**

   Teacher Comment: **The next row shows four animals: a dog, a cat, a horse, and a zebra. Which animal is brown?**
     Student Response: The dog is brown.
   Teacher Comment: **Circle the brown dog.**

   Teacher Comment: **The last row shows four animals: a shark, a chicken, a horse, and a cow. Which animal is brown?**
     Student Response: The cow is brown.
   Teacher Comment: **Circle the brown cow.**

© 2015 The Critical Thinking Co.™ • www.CriticalThinking.com • 800-458-4849

Kindergarten Thinking Skills & Key Concepts   Teacher's Manual

Thinking About Thinking
   Teacher Comment: **What did you pay attention to in order to find the right color?**
   Student Response:
   1. I paid attention to the color of the example.
   2. I looked for the same color.
   3. I named the shape or object that is the same color.

Personal Application
   Teacher Comment: **When do you have to name a color?**
   Student Response: I name a color to make requests (e.g. "Please hand me that red block, not the blue one.") or to give directions (e.g. "Wait until the light turns green.")

Page 9: DESCRIBING BLACK

LESSON

Stating the Objective
   Teacher Comment: **In this lesson you will identify the black object in each row.**

Conducting the Lesson
   Teacher Comment: **Name the shapes in the first row.**
      Student Response: The shapes are a triangle, a rectangle, a circle, and a hexagon.
   Teacher Comment: **Which shape is black?**
      Student Response: The rectangle is black.
   Teacher Comment: **Circle the black rectangle.**

   Teacher Comment: **Name the shapes in the second row.**
      Student Response: The shapes are a triangle, a square, a hexagon, and a circle.
   Teacher Comment: **Which shape is black?**
      Student Response: The circle is black.
   Teacher Comment: **Circle the black circle.**

   Teacher Comment: **The third row shows animals. Name the animals.**
      Student Response: The animals are a cat, a dog, a goat, and a camel.
   Teacher Comment: **Which animal is black?**
      Student Response: The cat is black.
   Teacher Comment: **Circle the black cat.**

   Teacher Comment: **The next row shows vehicles. Name these vehicles.**
      Student Response: The vehicles are a motorcycle, a tractor, a pickup truck, and a train.
   Teacher Comment: **Which vehicle is black?**
      Student Response: The pickup truck is black.
   Teacher Comment: **Circle the black pickup truck.**

   Teacher Comment: **The last row shows animals: a whale, a snake, a turtle, and a lizard. Which animal is black?**
      Student Response: The whale is black.
   Teacher Comment: **Circle the black whale.**

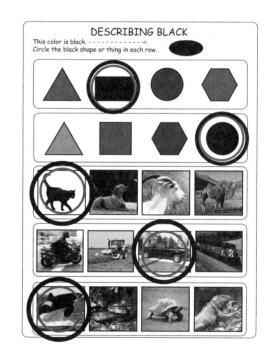

Thinking About Thinking
    Teacher Comment: **What did you pay attention to in order to find the right color?**
    Student Response:
        1. I paid attention to the color of the example.
        2. I looked for the same color.
        3. I named the shape or object that is the same color.

Personal Application
    Teacher Comment: **When do you have to name a color?**
    Student Response: I name a color to make requests (e.g. "Please hand me that red block, not the blue one.") or to give directions (e.g. "Wait until the light turns green.")

Page 10: DESCRIBING WHITE

LESSON

Stating the Objective
    Teacher Comment: **In this lesson we will identify the white object in each row.**

Conducting the Lesson
    Teacher Comment: **Name the shapes in the first row.**
        Student Response: The shapes are a rectangle, a circle, a triangle, and a hexagon.
    Teacher Comment: **Which shape is white?**
        Student Response: The triangle is white.
    Teacher Comment: **Circle the white triangle.**

    Teacher Comment: **Name the shapes in the second row.**
        Student Response: The shapes are a square, a hexagon, a triangle and a circle.
    Teacher Comment: **Which shape is white?**
        Student Response: The hexagon is white.
    Teacher Comment: **Circle the white hexagon.**

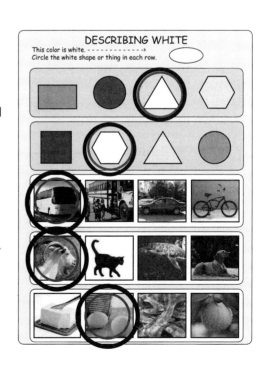

    Teacher Comment: **The third row shows vehicles. Name the vehicles.**
        Student Response: The vehicles are a bus, a school bus, a car, and a bicycle.
    Teacher Comment: **Which vehicle is white?**
        Student Response: The bus is white.
    Teacher Comment: **Circle the white bus.**

    Teacher Comment: **The next row shows animals. Name the animals.**
        Student Response: The animals are a goat, cat, a shark, and a dog.
    Teacher Comment: **Which animal is white?**
        Student Response: The goat is white.
    Teacher Comment: **Circle the white goat.**

Kindergarten Thinking Skills & Key Concepts   Teacher's Manual

   Teacher Comment: **The next row shows foods we eat for breakfast. Name these foods.**
      Student Response: The foods are butter, eggs, bacon, and an orange.
   Teacher Comment: **Which food is white?**
      Student Response: The eggs are white.
   Teacher Comment: **Circle the white eggs.**

Thinking About Thinking
   Teacher Comment: **What did you pay attention to in order to find the right color?**
      Student Response:
         1. I paid attention to the color of the example.
         2. I looked for the same color.
         3. I named the shape or object that is the same color.

Personal Application
   Teacher Comment: **When do you have to name a color?**
      Student Response: I name a color to make requests (e.g. "Please hand me that red block, not the blue one.") or to give directions (e.g. "Wait until the light turns green.")

Pages 11-12: NAMING COLORS

LESSON

Introduction
In previous lessons we have identified the colors red, orange, yellow, green, blue, purple, brown, black, and white.

Stating the Objective
   Teacher Comment: **In this lesson you will trace and write the names of the eight colors we have been studying.**

Conducting the Lesson
   Teacher Comment: **What are the colors on page 11?**
      Student Response: The colors are red, orange, yellow, and green.
   Teacher Comment: **The word for each color is shown beside it. Trace each word and then copy it.**

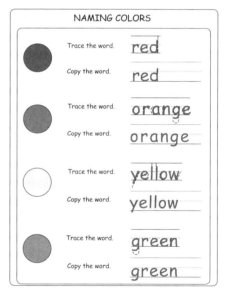

Thinking About Thinking
   Teacher Comment: **What did you pay attention to when you traced and copied the words?**
      Student Response:
         1. I thought about the sound of each letter as I copied it.
         2. I wrote each letter to match the one I traced.

Personal Application
   Teacher Comment: **When do you need to know how to write the names of colors?**
      Student Response: I need to know how to write the names of colors when I need to describe something.

Teaching Suggestion: Repeat this process for the colors on page 12.

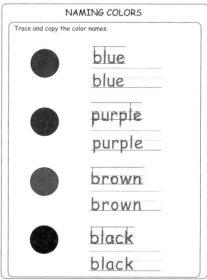

Pages 13-14: MATCHING PICTURES TO COLORS

LESSON

Introduction
   Teacher Comment: **In the first color lessons we thought about one color at a time. Then we learned to write the names of the colors.**

Stating the Objective
   Teacher Comment: **In this lesson you will match each picture to the name of the color of the object.**

Conducting the Lesson
   Teacher Comment: **Notice that a line has been drawn from the picture of the grapes to the word "purple." What is the object in the second picture?**
      Student Response: That picture shows corn.
   Teacher Comment: **What color is the corn?**
      Student Response: The corn is yellow.
   Teacher Comment: **Draw a line from the corn to the word "yellow."**

Teaching Suggestion: Repeat this process for the rest of the pictures.

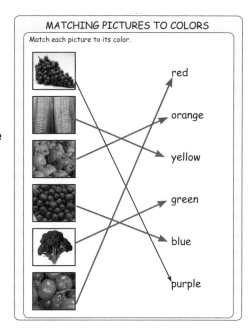

Thinking About Thinking
   Teacher Comment: **What did you pay attention to when you traced and copied the words?**
      Student Response:
      1. I found the name of the color of the object in the picture.
      2. I checked that the picture matched the word for the color.

Personal Application
   Teacher Comment: **When do you need to know how to recognize the words for colors?**
      Student Response: I need to know how to read the names of colors on notes, in books, and on packages.

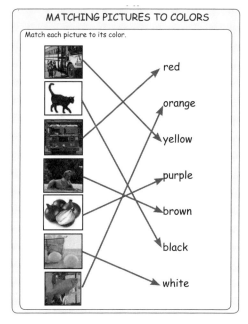

CHAPTER TWO – DESCRIBING SHAPES (Pages 16-43)

TEACHING ABOUT SHAPES

CURRICULUM APPLICATIONS
Language Arts: Visual discrimination for reading readiness
Mathematics: Naming geometric shapes
Science: Recognizing shapes of leaves, insects, or shells
Social Studies: Recognizing geographic features on map puzzles
Enrichment Areas: Recognizing shapes of road signs; describing patterns in art

LANGUAGE INTEGRATION ACTIVITIES
- Ask students to cut out pictures of objects that are good examples of the shapes discussed in this chapter. Organize their pictures into a bulletin board display, grouping and labeling the objects by shape.

TEACHING SUGGESTIONS
- Ask students to discuss and explain their answers in complete sentences. When asked, "How many sides does a square have?," A student may correctly answer "four." If the student responds, "A square has four sides," he or she has named the shape and its characteristics, imprinting the term for its shape and stating its properties. This practice seems artificial at first, but it is essential for young children, especially second-language learners.
- Ask students to name the object as they discuss it and explain their answers.
- Integrate these shape terms into your language arts program by discussing picture books which emphasize shape.
- In many of these lessons the teacher directions to students include language that shows order (first ..., next...., last; first ..., second ..., third ...., last). Many young students may not be familiar with these terms in the kind of directions used in school. Repetition of these sequences and consequently hearing them in student responses models the language patterns that students will need in primary grade writing tasks.
- At the end of the chapter, apply lines and curves to writing the alphabet.
- Some lessons conclude by asking students to create a drawing that contains the polygon featured in the lesson. For additional directions on drawing objects that contain various shapes consult *Ed Emberley's Drawing Book: Make a World,* ISBN 0316789720.

Page 16: DESCRIBING LINES

LESSON

Introduction
Lines are thin marks. We see lines all around us. They are the edges of shapes or objects like wires, jump ropes, or rubber bands. They can be any color.

Stating the Objective
    Teacher Comment: **Lines are thin marks that can be any color. Some lines are long. Some lines are short. Some lines are straight. Some lines are curved. In this lesson you will identify lines and color them.**

Conducting the Lesson
    Teacher Comment: **In the top box trace and color the line green.**
    Teacher Comment: **Lines can be different colors. Trace and color these lines to match the colors.**
    Teacher Comment: **Lines can point in any direction. Trace and color the lines purple.**
    Teacher Comment: **Lines can be different lengths. The length of a line is long or short compared to other lines. Look at the box at the bottom of the page. Color the short lines green.**
    Teacher Comment: **Now color the long lines red.**

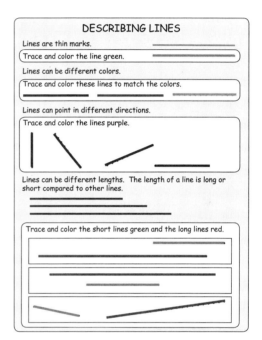

- Check students' work. Continue this dialog to discuss students' answers.

Thinking About Thinking
    Teacher Comment: **What did you pay attention to when you colored the lines?**
    Student Response:
    1. I looked at both lines.
    2. I decided which line was longer than the other.
    3. I held my hand steady to make the line straight.

Personal Application
    Teacher Comment: **When do you need to draw long or short lines?**
    Student Response: I need to draw long or short lines when I write letters or draw pictures.

Pages 17: DESCRIBING LINES

Introduction
Lines are thin marks. They can be any color.

Stating the Objective
    Teacher Comment: **In this lesson you will show which lines are straight and which are curved.**

Conducting the Lesson
    Teacher Comment: **Look at the straight line that is colored green. Remember how it feels to draw a straight line. You held you hand steady to be sure that the line did not bend. Look at the lines that are colored red. To color the bends in those lines, you must be careful to follow the curve in the line. Trace and color the straight lines with your green crayon. Color the curved lines with your red crayon.**

- Check students' work.

Thinking About Thinking

Teacher Comment: **What did you pay attention to when you colored the lines?**

Student Response:
1. I decided whether the line was straight or curved.
2. I picked the color to show straight or curved.
3. I held my hand steady to make the lines straight or follow the curve.

Personal Application

Teacher Comment: **When do you need to draw straight or curved lines?**

Student Response: I need to draw straight or curved lines when I write letters or draw pictures.

- If students have practiced writing letters of the alphabet, review straight and curved lines in writing each letter. If they have not practiced writing letters, remember to use the terms "straight" or "curved" as you demonstrate writing each letter.

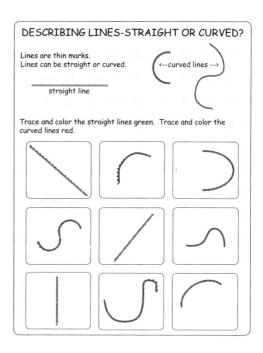

Page 18: DESCRIBING CIRCLES

LESSON

Introduction

- Hold up a circle.

  Teacher Comment: **We have practiced drawing a curve. A circle is a curve that has no beginning or end.**

- Use your finger to trace the edge of the circle a few times.

  Teacher Comment: **A circle looks the same from any side.**

- Mark a spot on the edge of the circle and rotate the circle twice.

  Teacher Comment: **Notice that however I turn the circle, it always looks the same. What are some objects that are shaped like a circle?**

Stating the Objective

Teacher Comment: **In this lesson you will show which shape is a circle.**

Conducting the Lesson

Teacher Comment: **What color is the circle in the first row?**
  Student Response: The circle in the first row is purple.
Teacher Comment: **Draw a circle around it.**
Teacher Comment: **What color is the circle in the second row?**
  Student Response: The circle in the second row is brown.
Teacher Comment: **Draw a circle around it.**
Teacher Comment: **What color is the circle in the third row?**
  Student Response: The circle in the third row is orange.
Teacher Comment: **Draw a circle around it.**

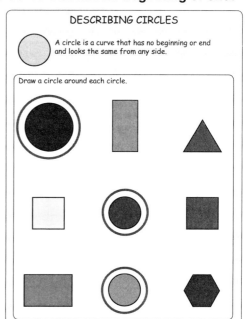

- Check students' work.

Thinking About Thinking
Teacher Comment: **What did you pay attention to when you looked for the circles?**
Student Response:
1. I paid attention to whether the shape had straight lines.
2. If the shape had straight lines, it was not a circle.
3. I looked for a curved line that looks the same from any side.

Personal Application
Teacher Comment: **When do you need to look for circles?**
Student Response: I look for circles to draw things or find things that are shaped like a circle.

Page 19: FINDING CIRCLES

LESSON

Introduction
- Hold up a circle.
  Teacher Comment: **We have practiced finding circles.**

Stating the Objective
Teacher Comment: **In this lesson you will find the circles in photographs and trace them.**

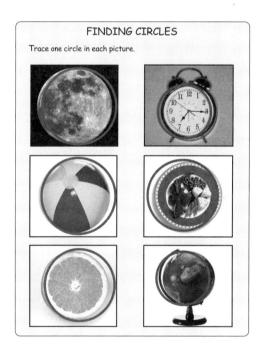

Conducting the Lesson
Teacher Comment: **In the first photograph we see the moon.**
Teacher Comment: **Trace the circle that you see on the moon.**
Teacher Comment: **The second picture shows a clock. Trace the circle.**
Teacher Comment: **The next picture shows a ball. Trace the circle.**
Teacher Comment: **The next picture shows a plate. Trace the circle.**
Teacher Comment: **The next picture shows an orange. Trace the circle.**
Teacher Comment: **The last picture shows a globe. A globe is a map that shows the land and the water on the earth. Trace the circle.**

Thinking About Thinking
Teacher Comment: **What did you pay attention to when you traced the circles?**
Student Response:
1. I found the circle in the picture.
2. I kept my crayon along the edge of the circle.

Personal Application
Teacher Comment: **When do you need to find a circle in an object?**
Student response: I need find a circle to draw an object that has a circle in it.

Kindergarten Thinking Skills & Key Concepts   Teacher's Manual

Page 20: DRAWING CIRCLES

LESSON

Introduction
- Hold up a circle.

   Teacher Comment: **We have found circles in pictures.**

Stating the Objective
   Teacher Comment: **In this lesson you will trace and color circles.**

Conducting the Lesson
   Teacher Comment: **Trace the word "circle." Trace each circle. Pay attention to how it feels to close a circle. Color the inside of each circle with any color that you choose.**

- Check students' work.

Thinking About Thinking
   Teacher Comment: **What did you pay attention to when you traced the circles?**
   Student Response:
   1. I was careful to make my line follow the curve.
   2. I paid attention to how it feels to close the circle.

Personal Application
   Teacher Comment: **When do you need to draw circles?**
   Student response: I need to draw circles when I draw wheels, balls, or any other round shape.
- Give students a blank sheet of paper and ask them to draw a circle. Then ask them to draw a picture of something that contains a circle.

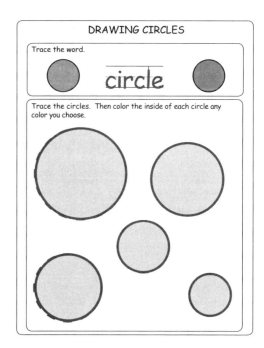

Page 21: DESCRIBING OVALS

LESSON

Introduction
- Hold up a circle.
  Teacher Comment: **We have drawn circles. We know that a circle looks the same when I turn it.**
- Rotate the circle. Hold up an oval beside it.
  Teacher Comment: **This shape is an oval. Notice that the oval looks different from a circle.**
- Put down the circle. Use your finger to trace the edge of the oval a few times.
  Teacher Comment: **Notice that the oval is also a curve that has no beginning or end. It looks like a flattened circle.**
- Mark a spot on the edge of the oval and rotate it twice.
  Teacher Comment: **Notice that when I turn the oval, it looks longer in different directions.**

Stating the Objective
  Teacher Comment: **In this lesson you will find ovals - shapes that look like a flattened circle.**

Conducting the Lesson
  Teacher Comment: **What color is the oval in the top row?**
    Student Response: The oval is green.
  Teacher Comment: **Draw a circle around it.**
  Teacher Comment: **What color is the oval in the second row?**
    Student Response: The oval in the second row is blue.
  Teacher Comment: **Draw a circle around it.**
  Teacher Comment: **What colors are the ovals in the third row?**
    Student Response: One oval is red. The other oval is orange.
  Teacher Comment: **Draw circles around them.**

- Check students' work.

  Teacher Comment: **Trace the dotted oval. Color it any color that you choose. Trace the oval that you see in each picture.**

- Check students' work.

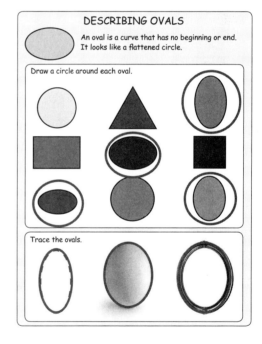

Thinking About Thinking
  Teacher Comment: **What did you pay attention to when you looked for ovals?**
    Student response:
    1. I looked for shapes that do not look the same all the way around.
    2. I found the oval.
    3. When I traced the oval, I kept my crayon along the edge.

Personal Application
  Teacher Comment: **When do you need to find or draw ovals?**
    Student response: I need to find or draw ovals when I draw faces or other objects that are oval.
- Give students a sheet of paper on which you have drawn a vertical oval. Ask students to draw and color a face on the oval.

Page 22: DESCRIBING ANGLES - LINES THAT TOUCH

LESSON

Introduction
- Hold up two rulers.
  Teacher Comment: **When two straight lines touch, they form an angle.**

- Put the rulers together to form an acute angle.
  Teacher Comment: **The angle can be sharp like this one.**

- Move the rulers to form a right angle.
  Teacher Comment: **The angle can look like a square corner.**

- Move the rulers to form an obtuse angle.
  Teacher Comment: **The angle can be wide like this one.**

Stating the Objective
  Teacher Comment: **In this lesson you will find lines that touch to make angles.**

Conducting the Lesson
  Teacher Comment: **Which lines in the first row touch to make an angle?**
    Student Response: The green and blue lines make an angle.
  Teacher Comment: **Notice a circle is drawn around it.**
  Teacher Comment: **Which lines in the second row touch to make an angle?**
    Student Response: The yellow and blue lines make an angle. The pink and the green lines make an angle.
  Teacher Comment: **Draw circles around the angles.**

- Check students' work.

  Teacher Comment: **When straight lines touch on all corners, they form shapes. Trace the shapes.**

Thinking About Thinking
  Teacher Comment: **What did you pay attention to when you looked for angles?**
    Student response:
    1. I looked for lines that touched.
    2. I saw that when straight lines touched on all corners, they form shapes.

Personal Application
  Teacher Comment: **When do you need to find angles?**
    Student response: I need to find angles when I draw objects with angles such as roofs, tents, boxes, doors, windows, etc.

Page 23: DESCRIBING SQUARES

LESSON

Introduction
- Hold up a square.
  Teacher Comment: **In the last lesson we learned that when lines touch, they make an angle.**

- Run your finger along the side of the square
  Teacher Comment: **Each side of this shape is a straight line. Notice that all sides are the same length.**

- Run your finger along each side to show that they are the same length.
  Teacher Comment: **Where two sides touch, they form an angle.**

- Run your finger along the corner.
  Teacher Comment: **Each angle is a square corner. What do we call this shape?**
  Student Response: That shape is a square.
  Teacher Comment: **How many sides does a square have?**
  Student response: A square has four sides.
  Teacher Comment: **How many angles does the square have?**
  Student response: A square has four angles.

- Rotate the square
  Teacher Comment: **Notice that the square is still a square when I turn it.**

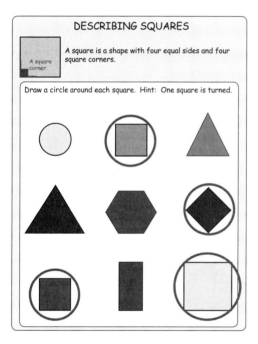

Stating the Objective
  Teacher Comment: **In this lesson you will circle the squares in each group of shapes. Be sure that all sides of the shape are the same length.**

Conducting the Lesson
  Teacher Comment: **What color is the square in the first row?**
  Student Response: The square is orange.
  Teacher Comment: **Circle the orange square. What color is the square in the second row?**
  Student Response: The square is blue.
  Teacher Comment: **Circle the blue square. What color are the squares in the third row?**
  Student Response: One square is red, the other is yellow.
  Teacher Comment: **Circle the squares.**

Thinking About Thinking
  Teacher Comment: **What did you pay attention to when you looked for the squares?**
  Student Response:
  1. I paid attention to whether the shape had four straight lines.
  2. I saw that all the sides are the same length.
  3. I made sure that the angles were square corners.

Personal Application
  Teacher Comment: **When do you need to find squares?**
  Student response: I need to find squares in objects in order to draw them correctly.

Page 24: FINDING SQUARES

LESSON

Introduction
- Hold up a square

   Teacher Comment: **We know that squares have four sides and four angles.**

Stating the Objective
   Teacher Comment: **We have found squares in our room and on paper. In this lesson you will look at photographs that show objects that are square. You will trace the squares that you see.**

Conducting the Lesson
   Teacher Comment: **In the first photograph we see a traffic sign. What shape is it?**
      Student Response: The traffic sign is square.
   Teacher Comment: **Trace the square.**
   Teacher Comment: **The second picture shows a present. Trace a square.**
   Teacher Comment: **The next picture shows a quilt. A quilt is a large bed covering that is made of many small pieces of cloth. Trace a square.**
   Teacher Comment: **The next picture shows floor tiles. Trace a square.**
   Teacher Comment: **The next picture shows a sign that tells a driver that an airport is nearby. Trace the square.**
   Teacher Comment: **The last picture shows a picture frame. Trace the square.**

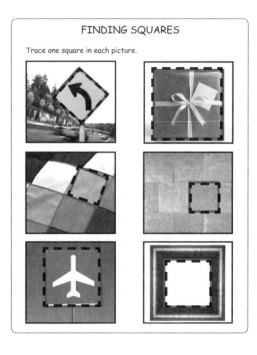

- Check students' work.

Thinking About Thinking
   Teacher Comment: **What did you pay attention to when you traced the squares?**
   Student Response:
   1. I paid attention to whether the shape had four straight sides and four square corners.
   2. I made sure that all the sides were the same length.
   3. I was careful kept my crayon on each straight line and each square corner.

Personal Application
   Teacher Comment: **When do you need to find a square?**
   Student response: I need to find a square in an object in order to draw it correctly.

Page 25: DRAWING SQUARES

LESSON

Introduction
- Hold up a square

    Teacher Comment: **We have found squares in objects.**

Stating the Objective
    Teacher Comment: **In the lesson you will trace and color squares.**

Conducting the Lesson
    Teacher Comment: **Trace the word "square."**

    Teacher Comment: **Trace each square. Pay attention to how it feels to draw each straight side and square corner. Color the inside of each square with any color that you choose.**

- Check students' work.

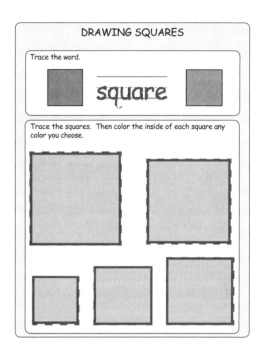

Thinking About Thinking
    Teacher Comment: **What did you pay attention to when you traced the squares?**
    Student Response:
    1. I was careful to trace straight lines.
    2. I was careful to trace square corners.
    3. I remembered how it feels to trace a square.

Personal Application
    Teacher Comment: **When do you need to draw squares?**
    Student response: I need to draw squares when I draw boxes, windows, and other square things.

- Give students a blank sheet of paper and ask them to draw a square. Then ask them to draw a picture of something that contains a square.

Page 26: DESCRIBING RECTANGLES

LESSON

Introduction
- Hold up a rectangle and a square.

    Teacher Comment: **How is a rectangle like a square?**
    Student Response: A rectangle has four sides and four angles like a square.
    Teacher Comment: **How is a rectangle different from a square?**
    Student Response: In a rectangle two sides are longer than the other two.

Stating the Objective
    Teacher Comment: **In this lesson you will show which shape is a rectangle.**

Kindergarten Thinking Skills & Key Concepts   Teacher's Manual

Conducting the Lesson
　　Teacher Comment: **A rectangle is a shape with four sides and four square corners. A rectangle has two sides that are longer than the other two sides. What color is the rectangle in the first row?**
　　　Student Response: The rectangle is orange.
　　Teacher Comment: **Draw a circle around the orange rectangle. Circle all the rectangles in the top box**

- Check students' work.

　　Teacher Comment: **When two of the sides are longer, we call the shape a rectangle. When all the sides are equal, we call that shape a square. Color the squares blue. Use an orange crayon to color the rectangles that are not squares.**

- Check students' work.

Thinking About Thinking
　　Teacher Comment: **What did you pay attention to when you looked for the rectangles?**
　　　Student Response:
　　　1. I paid attention to whether the shape had four straight lines.
　　　2. I made sure that the corners were square.
　　　3. I saw that two sides are longer than the other two.

　　Teacher Comment: **How did you tell the difference between the squares and other rectangles.**
　　　Student response: The sides of the square are all the same. Two sides of the rectangles are longer than the other two.

Personal Application
　　Teacher Comment: **When do you need to find rectangles?**
　　　Student response: I need to find rectangles in order to draw objects such as doors, windows, and pictures.

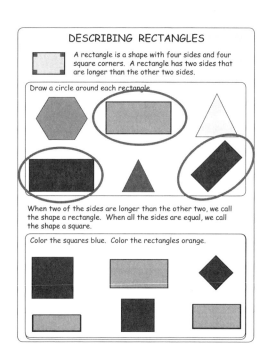

Page 27: FINDING RECTANGLES

LESSON

Introduction
　　Teacher Comment: **We have practiced finding rectangles.**

Stating the Objective
　　Teacher Comment: **In this lesson you will find rectangles in photographs and trace them.**

Conducting the Lesson
　　Teacher Comment: **In the first photograph there are many bricks. What shape are they?**
　　　Student Response: The bricks are rectangles
　　Teacher Comment: **Trace one rectangle.**
　　Teacher Comment: **The second picture shows a window. Trace a rectangle.**

Kindergarten Thinking Skills & Key Concepts — Teacher's Manual

Teacher Comment: **The next picture shows a picture frame. Trace a rectangle.**
Teacher Comment: **The next picture shows an elevator. Trace a rectangle.**
Teacher Comment: **The next picture shows a pizza that has been baked in a pan that is a rectangle. Trace the rectangle.**
Teacher Comment: **The last picture shows the keypad of a telephone. Trace a rectangle.**

- Check students' work.

Thinking About Thinking
Teacher Comment: **What did you pay attention to when you traced the rectangles?**
Student Response:
1. I found a rectangle in the picture.
2. I was careful to draw straight sides and square corners.

Personal Application
Teacher Comment: **When do you need to find rectangles?**
Student response: I need to find rectangles when I need to draw boxes, windows or other things that show rectangles.

Page 28: DRAWING RECTANGLES

LESSON

Introduction
Teacher Comment: **We have found and traced rectangles in photographs.**

Stating the Objective
In this lesson you will trace some rectangles.

Conducting the Lesson
Teacher Comment: **Trace the word "rectangle."**
Teacher Comment: **Trace each rectangle. Pay attention to how it feels to draw each straight side and square corner. Color the inside of each rectangle with any color that you choose.**

- Check students' work.

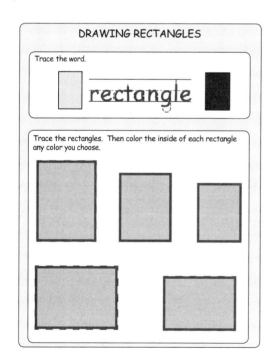

Thinking About Thinking
Teacher Comment: **What did you pay attention to when you traced the rectangles?**
Student Response:
1. I was careful to trace straight lines.
2. I was careful to trace square corners.
3. I remembered how it feels to trace a square.

Personal Application
Teacher Comment: **When do you need to draw rectangles?**
Student response: I need to draw rectangles when I draw boxes, windows, and other things that are rectangles.

- Give students a blank sheet of paper and ask them to draw a rectangle. Then ask them to draw a picture of something that contains a rectangle.

Kindergarten Thinking Skills & Key Concepts   Teacher's Manual

Page 29: DESCRIBING TRIANGLES

LESSON

Introduction
- Hold up a triangle.
    Teacher Comment: **What do we call this shape?**
        Student Response: That shape is a triangle.
    Teacher Comment: **How many sides does a triangle have?**
        Student response: A triangle has three sides.
    Teacher Comment: **How many corners called angles does the triangle have?**
        Student response: A triangle has three angles.

Stating the Objective
    Teacher Comment: **You know that triangles have three straight lines and three angles. In this lesson you will circle the triangles in a group of shapes.**

Conducting the Lesson
    Teacher Comment: **Name the shapes in the first row.**
        Student Response: The first row has a circle, a square, and a circle.
    Teacher Comment: **What colors are the triangles in the second row?**
        Student Response: One triangle is orange and the other is yellow.
    Teacher Comment: **How are the triangles different?**
        Student Response: The triangles have different colors and point in different directions.
    Teacher Comment: **Draw circles around the triangles.**
    Teacher Comment: **What colors are the triangles in the third row?**
        Student Response: One triangle is green and the other is purple.
    Teacher Comment: **How are the triangles different?**
        Student Response: One triangle is small and the other is large.
    Teacher Comment: **Draw circles around the triangles.**

Thinking About Thinking
    Teacher Comment: **What did you pay attention to when you found the triangles?**
        Student Response:
            1. I paid attention to whether the shape had three straight lines.
            2. I counted the three angles.

Personal Application
    Teacher Comment: **When do you need to find triangles?**
        Student response: I need to find triangles when I draw an object that has triangles.

Kindergarten Thinking Skills & Key Concepts — Teacher's Manual

Page 30: FINDING TRIANGLES

LESSON

Introduction
   Teacher Comment: **We have found triangles in a group of shapes.**

Stating the Objective
   Teacher Comment: **In this lesson you will find triangles in photographs and trace them.**

Conducting the Lesson
   Teacher Comment: **In the first photograph we see a very old building. It is called a pyramid. What shape is it?**
      Student Response: The pyramid is a triangle.
   Teacher Comment: **Trace the triangle.**
   Teacher Comment: **The second picture shows the top of a house. Find and trace a triangle.**
   Teacher Comment: **The next picture shows a napkin that is folded. Trace the triangle.**
   Teacher Comment: **The next picture shows a traffic sign. Trace the triangle.**
   Teacher Comment: **The next picture shows a sandwich that is cut into a triangle. Trace the triangle.**
   Teacher Comment: **The next picture shows a musical instrument that makes a sound like a bell. It is called a triangle. Trace the triangle.**

- Check students' work.

Thinking About Thinking
   Teacher Comment: **What did you pay attention to in order to find the triangles?**
      Student Response:
      1. I looked carefully for three straight lines.
      2. I was careful to draw straight lines.
      3. I traced the angles carefully.

Personal Application
   Teacher Comment: **When do you need to find triangles?**
      Student response: I need to find triangles when I draw an object that has triangles.

Kindergarten Thinking Skills & Key Concepts — Teacher's Manual

Page 31: DRAWING TRIANGLES

LESSON

Introduction
　Teacher Comment: **We have found triangles in a group of shapes. We traced triangles shown in drawings and photographs.**

Stating the Objective
　Teacher Comment: **In this lesson you will trace and color four triangles.**

Conducting the Lesson
　Teacher Comment: **Trace the word "triangle." Trace each triangle. Pay attention to how it feels to draw each straight side. Pay attention to how it feels when you draw sharp angles, square angles, and wide angles. Color the inside of each triangle with any color that you choose.**

- Check students' work.

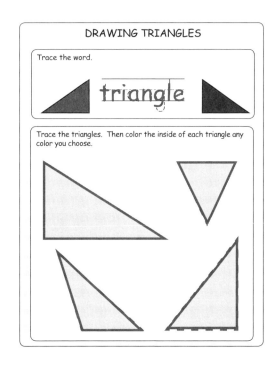

Thinking About Thinking
　Teacher Comment: **What did you pay attention to when you traced the triangles?**
　　Student Response:
　　1. I was careful to trace straight lines.
　　2. I was careful to trace sharp, square, and wide angles.
　　3. I remembered how it feels to trace a triangle.

Personal Application
　Teacher Comment: **When do you need to draw triangles?**
　　Student response: I need to draw triangles when I draw houses, sailboats, ice cream cones, and other objects that have triangles.

- Give students a blank sheet of paper and ask them to draw a triangle. Then ask them to draw a picture of something that contains a triangle.

Page 32: DESCRIBING HEXAGONS

LESSON

Introduction
- Hold up a hexagon.
　Teacher Comment: **This shape is called a hexagon. Count with me as I touch each side. How many sides did we count?**
　　Student Response: The hexagon has six sides.
　Teacher Comment: **How many angles does a hexagon have?**
　　Student response: A hexagon has six angles.

Stating the Objective
　Teacher Comment: **In this lesson you will find the hexagons in a group of shapes.**

Kindergarten Thinking Skills & Key Concepts   Teacher's Manual

Conducting the Lesson

Teacher Comment: **Name the shapes in the first row.**
Student response: The first row has a red rectangle, a purple hexagon, and a yellow triangle.
Teacher Comment: **Draw a circle around the purple hexagon.**

Teacher Comment: **Name the shapes in the second row.**
Student response: The second row has an orange square, a red circle, and a blue hexagon.
Teacher Comment: **Draw a circle around the blue hexagon.**

Teacher Comment: **Name the shapes in the third row.**
Student response: The shapes are a green hexagon, a purple rectangle, and an orange hexagon.
Teacher Comment: **Circle the green hexagon and the orange hexagon.**

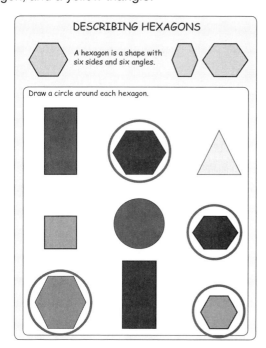

- Check students' work.

Thinking About Thinking

Teacher Comment: **What did you pay attention to when you found the hexagons?**
Student Response: I counted the number of sides to be sure that it had six.

Personal Application

Teacher Comment: **When do you need to find hexagons.**
Student response: I need to find hexagons when I draw an object that has hexagons.

Page 33: DRAWING HEXAGONS

LESSON

Introduction

Teacher Comment: **We have found hexagons in a group of shapes. Look at the orange hexagon. Because its sides are not equal, the orange hexagon looks flat. Look at the green hexagon. Because its sides are not equal, the green hexagon looks thin. If the sides of the hexagon are equal, it will look similar to a circle.**

Stating the Objective

Teacher Comment: **In this lesson you will trace and color four hexagons.**

Conducting the Lesson

Teacher Comment: **Trace each hexagon. Pay attention to how it feels to draw each straight side. Pay attention to how it feels when you draw sharp or wide angles.**

Teacher Comment: **Look at the hexagon that has equal sides. It is the hexagon that looks similar to a circle. Color it blue.**

Teacher Comment: **Color the other hexagons any color that you choose.**

- Check students' work.

Thinking About Thinking

Teacher Comment: **What did you pay attention to when you traced the hexagons?**

Student Response:
1. I was careful to trace straight lines.
2. I was careful to trace the wide angles.
3. I remembered how it feels to trace a hexagon.

Personal Application

Teacher Comment: **When do you need to draw hexagons?**

Student response: I need to draw hexagons when I draw objects that have hexagons.

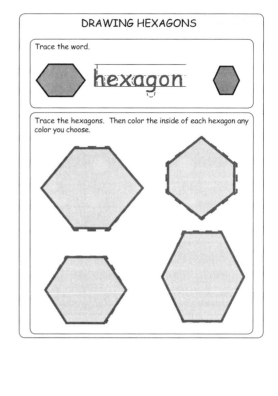

Page 34: TRACING SHAPES

LESSON

Introduction

Teacher Comment: **We have found different shapes in pictures.**

Stating the Objective

Teacher Comment: **In this lesson you will look at photographs that show one of the shapes that we have studied. You will trace the shape that you see in each picture.**

Conducting the Lesson

Teacher Comment: **What is the object that you see in the first picture?**
  Student Response: The object is a sign.
Teacher Comment: **What shape is the sign?**
  Student Response: The sign is a triangle.
Teacher Comment: **Trace the triangle.**

Teacher Comment: **What is the object that you see in the second picture?**
  Student Response: The object is a car license plate.
Teacher Comment: **What shape is the sign?**
  Student Response: The sign is a rectangle
Teacher Comment: **Trace the rectangle.**

Teacher Comment: **What is the object that you see in the third picture?**
  Student Response: The object is a television set.
Teacher Comment: **What shape is the television set?**
  Student Response: The television set is a rectangle.
Teacher Comment: **Trace the rectangle.**

Teacher Comment: **What is the object that you see in the fourth picture?**
  Student Response: The object is part of a bridge or a building.
Teacher Comment: **What shape is the part?**
  Student Response: The part is a triangle.
Teacher Comment: **Trace the triangle.**

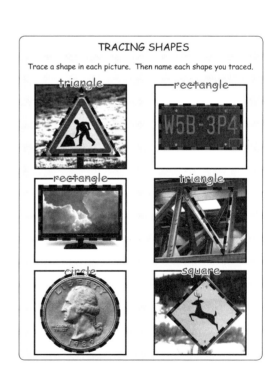

Kindergarten Thinking Skills & Key Concepts   Teacher's Manual

   Teacher Comment: **What is the object that you see in the fifth picture?**
      Student Response: The object is a quarter.
   Teacher Comment: **What shape is the quarter?**
      Student Response: The quarter is a circle.
   Teacher Comment: **Trace the circle.**

   Teacher Comment: **What is the object that you see in the last picture?**
      Student Response: The object is a sign.
   Teacher Comment: **What shape is the sign?**
      Student Response: The sign is a square.
   Teacher Comment: **Trace the square.**

• Check students' work.

Thinking About Thinking
   Teacher Comment: **What did you pay attention to in order to find the shapes?**
   Student Response:
      1. I looked carefully to decide the shape of the object.
      2. I named the shape.
      3. I was careful to draw straight or curved lines.
      4. I looked at the angles of the shape.

Personal Application
   Teacher Comment: **When do you need to find shapes?**
      Student response: I need to find shapes when I draw objects.

Page 35: MATCHING SHAPES AND COLORS

Introduction
   Teacher Comment: **We have studied shapes and colors.**

Stating the Objective
   Teacher Comment: **In this lesson you will match a shape to its color and its name.**

Conducting the Lesson
   Teacher Comment: **Look at page 35. What color is the hexagon at the top of the page?**
      Student Response: The hexagon is red.
   Teacher Comment: **Notice that a line has been drawn from the hexagon to the word "red." Also notice that another line is drawn from the hexagon to the word "hexagon." The first shape is a red hexagon.**
   Teacher Comment: **Name the second shape.**
      Student Response: The second shape is an orange triangle.
   Teacher Comment: **Draw a line from the triangle to the word "orange." Draw a line from the triangle to the word "triangle."**

• Repeat this dialog confirming that students respond with both the color and the shape.

• Check students' work.

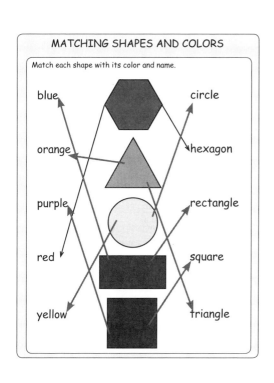

© 2015 The Critical Thinking Co.™ • www.CriticalThinking.com • 800-458-4849   29

Thinking About Thinking

Teacher Comment: **What did you pay attention to when you matched shapes to the words that describe their color and shape?**

Student Response:
1. I looked at a shape and named its color.
2. I looked down the list to find the word for the color.
3. I named its shape.
4. I looked down the list to find the word for its shape.
5. I described both the color and the shape.

Personal Application

Teacher Comment: **When do you need to name both the color and the shape of objects?**

Student response: I need to name both the color and the shape of things in order to tell about them.

Page 36: MATCHING SHAPES AND COLORS

LESSON

Introduction

Teacher Comment: **We have matched shapes and colors.**

Stating the Objective

Teacher Comment: **In this lesson we will match a picture to its color and shape.**
Teacher Comment: **Look at page 36. What color is the traffic sign in the first picture?**
    Student Response: The sign is red.
Teacher Comment: **Draw a line from the picture to the word "red."**
Teacher Comment: **What shape is the traffic sign?**
    Student Response: The sign is a triangle.
Teacher Comment: **Draw a line from the traffic sign to the word triangle.**

- Repeat this dialog for the rest of the pictures, naming the second, third, fourth, and last pictures. Check students' work.

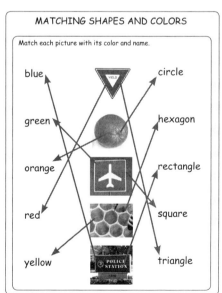

Thinking About Thinking

Teacher Comment: **What did you pay attention to when you matched shapes to the words that describe their color and shape?**

Student Response:
1. I looked at a shape and named its color.
2. I looked down the list to find the word for the color.
3. I named its shape.
4. I looked down the list to find the word for its shape.
5. I described both the color and the shape.

Personal Application

Teacher Comment: **When do you need to name both the color and the shape of objects?**

Student response: I need to name both the color and the shape of things in order to tell about them.

Pages 37-38: DESCRIBING SIZE

LESSON
- Read aloud the explanation and directions at the top of the page. Give students time to trace and copy the words.

Introduction
   Teacher Comment: **We have described shapes by color.**

Stating the Objective
   Teacher Comment: **In this lesson you will describe shapes by size.**

Conducting the Lesson
   Teacher Comment: **We call something "small" or "large" compared to each other. We call something "medium" if its size is between a small one and a large one. On page 37 trace and copy the words "small," "medium," and "large."**

- Check students' work.

   Teacher Comment: **We have written the words that describe size. On page 38 you will write an "S" on each small shape, an "M" on each medium shape, and an "L" on each large shape. In the first row notice that the letter "S" for small, "M" for medium, or "L" for large is written inside each yellow triangle.**
   Teacher Comment: **Describe the size, color, and shape of each one in the second row.**
      Student Response: In the second row there is a medium, pink circle, a large green square, and a small pink circle.
   Teacher Comment: **In the second row write "S," "M," or "L" to show the size of each shape.**

- Repeat this dialog for the third and fourth rows.

Thinking About Thinking
   Teacher Comment: **What did you pay attention to when you wrote the letters on each shape?**
   Student Response:
   1. I looked for the same shape.
   2. I found the small one and the large one.
   3. I then found the medium one by comparing it to the other two.

Personal Application
   Teacher Comment: **When do you need to name the size, color, and shape of objects?**
      Student response: I tell about size, color, and shape when I describe toys, bottles, bags, or food items.

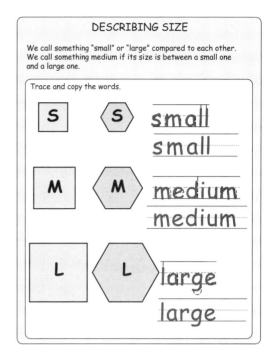

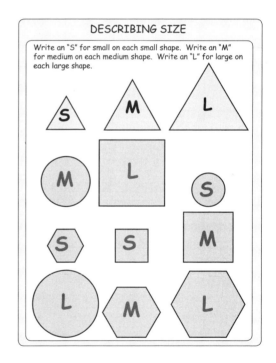

Page 39: DESCRIBING SOLIDS - CUBE AND SPHERE

LESSON

- Cut out the pattern for a cube.

  See the first graphic master in the appendix. Make three copies and cut out two. Construct a cube from one of them before you present the lesson.

Introduction
  Teacher Comment: **In the last lessons all the shapes were drawn on a piece of paper. Those shapes are flat. If the paper is folded correctly, some shapes will form a solid. A solid is an object that you can hold in your hand.**

Stating the Objective
  Teacher Comment: **In this lesson you will learn the names of two solids.**

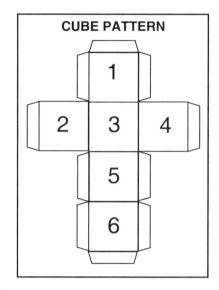

Conducting the Lesson
- Hold up the pattern for a cube.
  Teacher Comment: **On this piece of paper all the squares are flat.**

- Fold the pattern into a cube.
  Teacher Comment: **When I fold the piece of paper correctly, the flat paper becomes a solid.**

- Show the cube that you prepared and rotate it.
  Teacher Comment: **This solid is a cube. Notice that however I turn the cube, each side of the cube is a square. Let's count the number of squares.**

- Point to the number on each square as you count.
  Teacher Comment: **Trace and copy the word "cube."**

- Check students work.
  Teacher Comment: **Name the cubes in the pictures.**
    Student Response: The first picture shows ice cubes. The second picture shows a pair of dice.

- Hold up a flat sheet of paper with a circle drawn on it.
  Teacher Comment: **Notice that the circle is flat.**

- Crumple the circle into a tight ball.
  Teacher Comment: **Notice that the flat circle has become a solid that looks like a ball.**

- Hold up a ball and rotate it.
  Teacher Comment: Rotate the ball. **What does the ball look like in all directions.**
    Student Response: The ball looks like a circle any way you look at it.
  Teacher Comment: **This ball is a solid that is called a sphere. Trace and copy the word "sphere."**

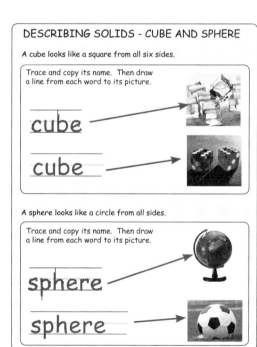

- Check students work.

  Teacher Comment: **Name the spheres in the pictures.**
    Student Response: The first picture shows a globe. The second picture shows a soccer ball.
  Teacher Comment: **Draw a line from each word to its picture.**

Thinking About Thinking
   Teacher Comment: **What did you pay attention to when you matched the word for the solid to the picture?**
   Student Response:
   1. I thought about the shape of the sides of the solid from each direction.
   2. I named the solid that has those shapes.
   3. I connected the word with the picture that shows that solid.

Personal Application
   Teacher Comment: **When do you need to know the words for different kinds of solids?**
   Student response: I need to know the words for solids in order to tell about them.

Page 40: DESCRIBING SOLIDS - CONE AND CYLINDER

LESSON

Introduction
   Teacher Comment: **In the last lesson we learned the names of two solids, the cube and the sphere.**

Stating the Objective
   Teacher Comment: **In this lesson you will learn the names of two more solids.**

Conducting the Lesson
- Twist a piece of colored paper into a cone. Cut the base so that it is flat to create a pattern for a cone.
- Hold up the flat pattern for the cone.
   Teacher Comment: **This piece of paper is flat. When I roll it into a solid, it becomes a cone. When you look at it from the side, what shape do you see?**
   Student Response: I see a triangle.
- Point the base toward the class.
   Teacher Comment: **When you look at the bottom, what shape so you see?**
   Student Response: The bottom is a circle.
   Teacher Comment: **Trace and copy the word "cone."**

- Check students work.

   Teacher Comment: **Name the cone in the first picture.**
   Student Response: The first picture shows an ice cream cone.
   Teacher Comment: **Draw a line from the word "cone" to the picture of the ice cream cone.**
   Teacher Comment: **The second picture shows a teepee. A teepee is an Indian tent.**
   Teacher Comment: **Draw a line from the word "cone" to the picture of the teepee.**

- Check students work.

- Roll a piece of colored paper into a cylinder.
- Hold up the flat pattern for the cylinder.
   Teacher Comment: **This piece of paper is flat. When I roll it into a solid, it becomes a cylinder. When you look at it from the side, what shape do you see?**
   Student Response: I see a rectangle.

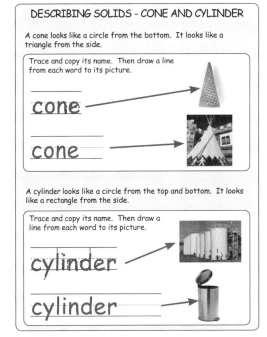

- Point the base toward the class.
    Teacher Comment: **When you look at the bottom, what shape so you see?**
        Student Response: The bottom is a circle.
    Teacher Comment: **Trace and copy the word "cylinder."**

- Check students work.

    Teacher Comment: **The buildings in the third picture are used to store grain. They are called silos. Draw a line from the word "cylinder" to the picture of the silos.**
    Teacher Comment: **Name the cylinder in the bottom picture.**
        Student Response: The bottom picture shows a trash can.
    Teacher Comment: **Draw a line from the word "cylinder" to the picture of the trash can.**

- Check students' work.

Thinking About Thinking
    Teacher Comment: **What did you pay attention to when you matched the word for the solid to the picture?**
    Student Response:
    1. I thought about the shape of the sides of the solid from each direction.
    2. I named the solid that has those shapes.
    3. I connected the word with the picture that shows that solid.

Personal Application
    Teacher Comment: **When do you need to know the words for different kinds of solids?**
        Student response: I need to know the words for solids in order to tell about them.

Page 41: DESCRIBING FLAT OR SOLID

LESSON

Introduction
    Teacher Comment: **In the last two lessons we learned the names of four solids: cube, sphere, cone, and cylinder.**

- Hold up examples asking students to name the object and the term for its shape.

Stating the Objective
    Teacher Comment: **In this lesson you will show the difference between flat shapes and solid objects.**

Conducting the Lesson
    Teacher Comment: **Circles, squares, rectangles, and triangles are flat objects. Cubes, spheres, cones, and cylinders are solids. Trace and copy the words "flat' and "solid."**

- Check students work.

    Teacher Comment: **Draw a line from each word to its picture.**

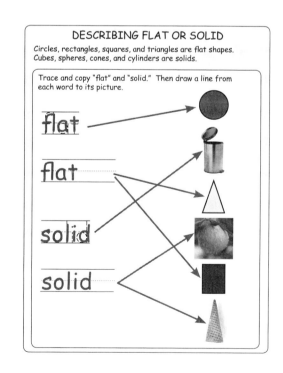

- Check students' work.

Thinking About Thinking
   Teacher Comment: **What did you pay attention to when you decided whether the pictures were flat or solid?**
   Student Response:
   1. I checked whether it was a real object or marks on paper.
   2. I connected the word to the picture.

Personal Application
   Teacher Comment: **When do you need to know whether a shape is flat or solid?**
   Student response: I need to know whether something is flat or solid to tell the difference between a drawing and a picture of a real thing.

Page 42: DESCRIBING SHAPES

LESSON
- Model the sentence pattern for describing shape and color. Encourage students to speak in whole sentences using this pattern with other polygons and objects.

Introduction
   Teacher Comment: **We have described shape and color.**

Stating the Objective
   Teacher Comment: **In this lesson you will complete descriptions of shapes.**

Conducting the Lesson
   Teacher Comment: **The example shows how we usually describe shapes. First we name the shape, then we name the color. Notice the dot at the end of the sentence. It is called a period. It tells the reader that you have finished. Trace the example.**

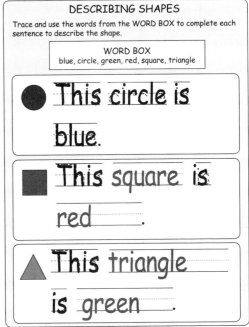

- Check students' work.

   Teacher Comment: **Use the words in the WORD BOX to finish sentences to describe the next two shapes.**

- Check students' work.

Thinking About Thinking
   Teacher Comment: **What did you pay attention to when you wrote a description of a shape?**
   Student Response:
   1. I named the shape and its color.
   2. I found the words for the shape and copied it. I found the word for its color and copied it.

Personal Application
   Teacher Comment: **When do you need to write about a shape?**
   Student Response: I need to tell the shape and color when I write a description of something.

Kindergarten Thinking Skills & Key Concepts — Teacher's Manual

Page 43: DESCRIBING SHAPES

LESSON

- Model the sentence pattern for describing shape, size, and color. Encourage students to speak in whole sentences using this pattern with other polygons and objects.

Introduction
  Teacher Comment: **We have described shapes and their color.**

Stating the Objective
  Teacher Comment: **In this lesson you will describe the size and color of shapes.**

Conducting the Lesson
  Teacher Comment: **The example shows how we usually describe the size and color of shapes. First we name the shape. Then we name the size. Then we name the color. Trace the example.**

- Check students' work.

  Teacher Comment: **Use the words in the WORD BOX to finish a sentence to describe each shape.**

- Check students' work.

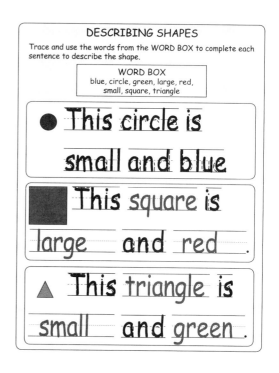

Thinking About Thinking
  Teacher Comment: **What did you pay attention to when you wrote a description of a shape?**
  Student Response:
  1. I named the shape, its size, and its color.
  2. I found the words for the shape and copied it. I found the word for its color and copied it.

Personal Application
  Teacher Comment: **When do you need to write about a shape?**
  Student Response: I need to tell the shape and color when I write a description of something.

CHAPTER THREE – SIMILARITIES AND DIFFERENCES IN SHAPES
(Pages 44-50)

GENERAL INTRODUCTION

CURRICULUM APPLICATIONS
Language Arts: Visual discrimination for reading readiness
Mathematics: Identify similar figures; write numerals in the correct direction (5, 7, etc.)
Science: Recognize similarly shaped leaves, insects, or shells
Social Studies: Match puzzle sections to geographic features on map puzzles
Enrichment Areas: Recognize shapes of road signs; discern patterns in art

TEACHING SUGGESTIONS
- Ask students to name the polygons and their properties as they discuss and explain their answers. Remember the words that students use to describe their choices. Use these same words to remind students of the key characteristics of items in these lessons.
- Integrate these geometry concepts into your language arts program by discussing picture books.
- Model using the sentence structure of comparison (both ... and) and contrast (but ... or). Encourage students to speak and write using those terms and patterns.

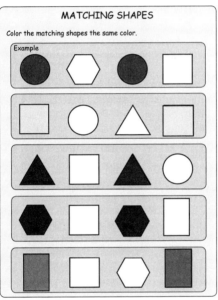

Pages 45-46: MATCHING SHAPES

LESSON

Introduction
  Teacher Comment: **In the last chapter we learned to describe shapes by size, shape and color.**

Stating the Objective
  Teacher Comment: **In this lesson you will find matching shapes and color them the same color.**

Conducting the Lesson
  Teacher Comment: **The first shape is a red circle. Notice that the third shape is also a red circle. The shapes that are the same are colored to match. Now look at the next row of shapes that starts with a yellow square. Color the matching shape the same color.**

Teaching Suggestion: Repeat this dialog for page 46.

Thinking About Thinking
  Teacher Comment: **What did you pay attention to when you matched these shapes?**
  Student Response:
    1. I looked carefully to find the shapes that match.
    2. I made them the same color.

Personal Application
  Teacher Comment: **When do you need to match shapes?**
  Student response: I need to match shapes when I put away toys or tools; match building blocks; match parts or sections from construction toys; or put away dishes or silverware.

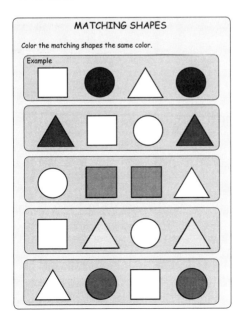

Kindergarten Thinking Skills & Key Concepts   Teacher's Manual

Pages 47-48: MATCHING BY SHAPE AND COLOR

LESSON

Introduction
   Teacher Comment: **In the last lesson we matched shapes that were the same and colored them.**

Stating the Objective
   Teacher Comment: **In this lesson you will match shapes that are the same color.**

Conducting the Lesson
   Teacher Comment: **Notice that a line has been drawn from the purple hexagon in the first column to the purple hexagon in the next column. Draw a line from the orange circle in the first column to the one that matches in the next column.**

- Check students' work.

   Teacher Comment: **Now draw lines from each shape to the one like it that has the same color.**

Teaching Suggestion: Repeat this dialog for page 48.

Thinking About Thinking
   Teacher Comment: **What did you pay attention to when you matched these shapes?**
   Student Response:
   1. I found the same shape.
   2. I checked that it is the same color.

Personal Application
   Teacher Comment: **When do you need to match shapes?**
   Student Response: I need to match shapes when I put away toys or tools; match building blocks; match parts or sections from construction toys; or put away dishes or silverware.

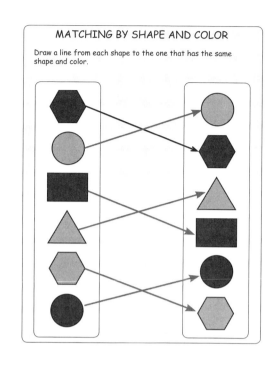

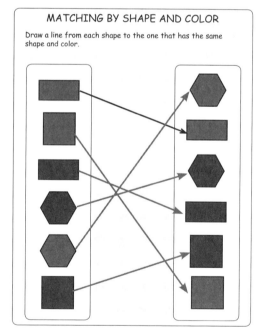

Page 49: HOW ALIKE?

LESSON

Introduction
   Teacher Comment: **Sometimes you must write about how shapes are alike.**

Stating the Objective
   Teacher Comment: **In this lesson you will complete sentences that describe how two shapes are alike.**

Conducting the Lesson
   Teacher Comment: **Notice that two words are missing from each sentence. As you trace the sentence, use the words in the WORD BOX to write in the missing words to explain how the shapes are alike.**

- Check students' work.

Thinking About Thinking
   Teacher Comment: **What did you pay attention to when you wrote how shapes are alike?**
   Student Response:
   1. I looked to see whether the shapes were the same color, same size, or same shape.
   2. I found the correct word and copied it.

Personal Application
   Teacher Comment: **When do you need to tell if shapes are alike?**
   Student response: I need to tell if shapes are alike when I make requests or give directions.

Page 50: HOW DIFFERENT?

LESSON

Introduction
Teacher Comment: **Sometimes you must write about how shapes are different.**

Stating the Objective
Teacher Comment: **In this lesson you will complete sentences that describe how two shapes are different.**

Conducting the Lesson
Teacher Comment: **Notice that two words are missing from the sentence. As you trace the sentence, use the words in the WORD BOX to write in the missing words to explain how the shapes are different.**

- Check students' work.

Thinking About Thinking
Teacher Comment: **What did you pay attention to when you wrote how shapes are different?**
Student Response:
1. I looked to see whether the shapes were different colors, different sizes, or different shapes.
2. I found the correct word and copied it.

Personal Application
Teacher Comment: **When do you need to tell if shapes are different?**
Student response: I need to tell if shapes are different when I make requests or give directions.

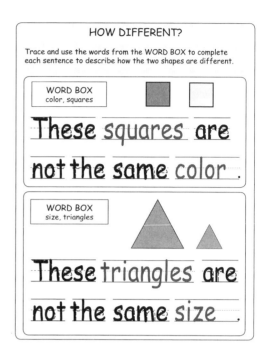

Kindergarten Thinking Skills & Key Concepts — Teacher's Manual

CHAPTER FOUR – SEQUENCES OF SHAPES (Pages 52-56)

GENERAL INTRODUCTION

CURRICULUM APPLICATIONS
Language Arts: Identify letter patterns in decoding unfamiliar words.
Mathematics: Identify repeating geometric patterns, simple bar graphs.
Science: Identify repeating patterns in leaves, shells, and life cycles.
Social Studies: Identify latitude and longitude.
Enrichment Areas: Art exercises involving patterns; repeating patterns in written music.

TEACHING SUGGESTIONS
- Check that students "read" the sequence of shapes from left to right.

Page 52 - WHAT COLOR SQUARE COMES NEXT?

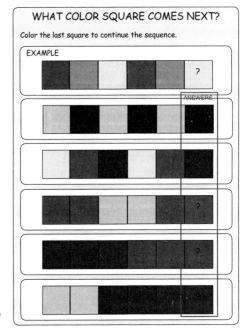

LESSON

Introduction
   Teacher Comment: **When the same shape or color is repeated, it becomes a sequence. When sequences are repeated many times, they make a pattern. Patterns are all around us in nature and in man-made things. Where in this room can you see examples of sequences?**
      Student Response: Examples may include fabric in clothing, brick or cement block walls, floor tiles, ceiling tiles, Venetian blinds, leaf arrangements on plants, etc.

Stating the Objective
   Teacher Comment: **In this lesson you will color the blank square to continue the sequence.**

Conducting the Lesson
   Teacher Comment: **Tell the color sequence that you see in the top row.**
      Student Response: The sequence is red, orange, yellow, red, orange, yellow.
   Teacher Comment: **The last square is colored yellow. This shows a completed sequence.**
   Teacher Comment: **Tell the color sequence in the second row.**
      Student Response: The sequence is green, black, green, black, green.
   Teacher Comment: **To continue the sequence, what color should the next square be?**
      Student Response: The last square should be black.

   Teacher Comment: **Find the sequence in each row, color the last square to continue the sequence.**

- Check students' work. Continue this dialog to discuss students' answers.

Thinking About Thinking
  Teacher Comment: **What did you pay attention to when you decided what color came next?**
  Student Response:
  1. I looked carefully at the colors of the squares.
  2. I looked for a sequence of colors.
  3. I figured out what the next color would be.

Personal Application:
  Teacher Comment: **When do you need to finish a sequence?**
  Possible Responses: I need to finish a sequence when I draw brick walls, leaves, floor or ceiling tiles, etc.

Page 53 - WHAT COLOR SQUARES COME NEXT?

LESSON

Introduction
  Teacher Comment: **In the last lesson we colored one square to continue a sequence.**

Stating the Objective
  Teacher Comment: **In this lesson you will also find a sequence and color two squares that continue the sequence.**

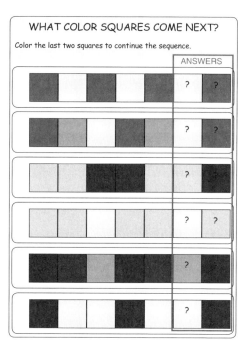

Conducting the Lesson
  Teacher Comment: **Let's say the color sequence that you see in the top row.**
   Student response: The sequence is red, yellow, red, yellow, red.
  Teacher Comment: **What should you color the next two squares?**
   Student response: The next square should be yellow and the last square should be red.
  Teacher Comment: **Color the last two squares to finish the sequence.**

- Check students' work. Continue this dialog to discuss students' answers.

Thinking About Thinking
  Teacher Comment: **What did you pay attention to when you decided what color came next?**
  Student Response:
  1. I looked carefully at the colors of the squares.
  2. I looked for a sequence of colors.
  3. I figured out what the next color would be.

Personal Application
  Teacher Comment: **When do you need to finish a sequence?**
  Possible Responses: I need to finish a sequence when I draw brick walls, leaves, floor or ceiling tiles, etc.

Page 54 - WHAT COMES NEXT?

LESSON

Introduction
  Teacher Comment: **In the last lesson we worked on completing a sequence of colors.**

Stating the Objective
  Teacher Comment: **In this exercise you will find the shape that completes the sequence using the shapes in the choice box.**

Conducting the Lesson
  Teacher Comment: **Tell the sequence of the shapes in the first row.**
    Student response: The sequence is red triangle, red hexagon, red square, green triangle, green hexagon.
  Teacher Comment: **Which shape comes next to continue the sequence?**
    Student response: The next shape should be a green square.
  Teacher Comment: **Notice that a line has been drawn from the green square to the first row. Now look at the second row. What is the sequence?**
    Student response: The sequence is blue circle, blue hexagon, blue square, purple circle, purple hexagon.
  Teacher Comment: **Which shape comes next?**
    Student response: The next shape should be a purple square.
  Teacher Comment: **Draw a line from the purple square in the choice box to its sequence.**

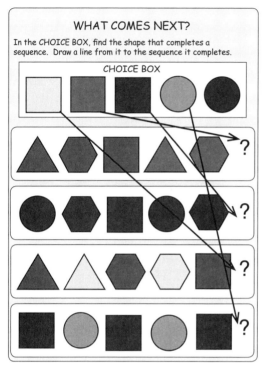

- Check students' work. Continue this dialog to discuss students' answers.

Thinking About Thinking
  Teacher Comment: **What did you pay attention to when you decided what shape came next?**
    Student response:
    1. I looked carefully at the colors and the shapes.
    2. I saw that the same sequence of color and shape was repeated.
    3. I figured out what the next one would be if the sequence continued.

Personal Application
  Teacher Comment: **When do you need to finish a sequence?**
    Possible Responses: I need to finish a sequence when I draw brick walls, leaves, floor or ceiling tiles, etc.

Teaching Suggestion: Repeat this dialog for page 55.

Page 56 - DESCRIBING A SEQUENCE

LESSON

Introduction
Teacher Comment: **In the last exercises we have described sequences of colors and shapes.**

Stating the Objective
Teacher Comment: **In this exercise you will complete a sentence that describes a sequence.**

Conducting the Lesson
Teacher Comment: **Describe the sequence you see.**
  Student response: I see a sequence of red square, green square, red square, green square, red square.

Thinking About Thinking
Teacher Comment: **What did you pay attention to when you traced the description?**
  Student response:
  1. I checked that all the shapes were squares.
  2. I checked the color sequence.

Personal Application
Teacher Comment: **When do you need to write a sequence?**
  Possible Responses: I need to write a sequence to write directions.

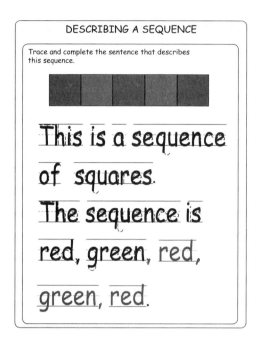

Kindergarten Thinking Skills & Key Concepts — Teacher's Manual

CHAPTER FIVE – KINDS OF SHAPES (Pages 58-68)
TEACHING KINDS OF SHAPES

CURRICULUM APPLICATIONS
Language Arts: Decoding in reading readiness; explaining kinds of shapes
Mathematics: Recognizing properties of polygons
Science: Classifying natural objects by shape (leaves, fish, shells, etc.)
Social Studies: Identifying road signs by their shape

Pages 58-59 - COMPARING CHARACTERISTICS

LESSON

Introduction
   Teacher Comment: **We have described how shapes are alike or different. We call ourselves a "class" of students. In this class everyone is about the same age, meets in the same place, studies the same things, and has the same teacher.** <u>Class</u> **means more than just a school room; it also means** <u>a group</u> **that** <u>has</u> **a** <u>common characteristic</u>. **When we describe the group by using that characteristic, we are** <u>classifying</u>.

Stating the Objective
   Teacher Comment: **In this lesson you will write "S" for "same" or "D" for "different" to show color, shape, and size.**

Conducting the Lesson
   Teacher Comment: **The example shows a large red square and a large blue hexagon. How are these shapes alike?**
      Student Response: They are both large.
   Teacher Comment: **Notice that an "S," for "same," is written on the size line.**
      Teacher Comment: **How are these shapes different?**
      Student Response: They are different colors and different shapes.
   Teacher Comment: **Notice that "D" for "different" is written on the "COLOR" line and on the "SHAPE" line.**
   Teacher Comment: **Look at the shapes in the second row. How are these shapes alike?**
      Student Response: They are both small shapes.

   Teacher Comment: **Write an "S" on the size line.**

   Teacher Comment: **How are these shapes different?**
      Student Response: They are different colors and different shapes.

   Teacher Comment: **With your partner mark how the shapes are different.**

• Check students' work. Continue this dialog to discuss students' answers.

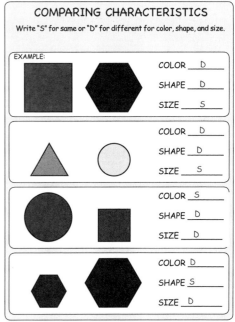

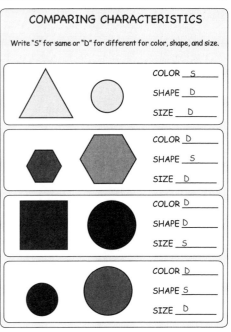

© 2015 The Critical Thinking Co.™ • www.CriticalThinking.com • 800-458-4849

45

Kindergarten Thinking Skills & Key Concepts   Teacher's Manual

Thinking About Thinking
  Teacher Comment: **What did you pay attention to in order to decide how to respond?**
  Student Response:
    1. I looked at the color characteristic.
    2. I looked at the shape characteristic.
    3. I looked at the size characteristic.

Personal Application
  Teacher Comment: **When do you need to pay attention to whether shape, color, or size are the same or different?**
  Student Response: I look for shape, color, or size when I match socks, do puzzles, or build with blocks.

Teaching Suggestion: Repeat this dialog for page 59.

Pages 60-62 - DESCRIBING A GROUP - WHAT BELONGS?

LESSON

Introduction
  Teacher Comment: **In the first lesson we described two shapes by color, shape, and size. Sometimes we group things by an important characteristic they all have. We call ourselves a "class" of students. In this class everyone is about the same age, meets in the same place, studies the same things, and has the same teacher. <u>Class</u> means more than just a school room; it also means <u>a group</u> <u>that</u> <u>has</u> <u>a</u> <u>common</u> <u>characteristic</u>. When we describe the group by using that characteristic, we are <u>classifying</u>.**

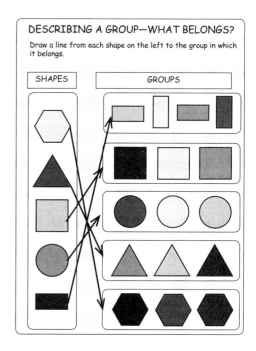

Stating the Objective
  Teacher Comment: **In this lesson you will match shapes to the group that has the same characteristics.**

Conducting the Lesson
  Teacher Comment: **Name the color and shape of the first shape.**
    Student Response: The shape is a yellow hexagon.
  Teacher Comment: **Notice that there is a line drawn to the group of hexagons. Name the color and shape of the second shape.**
    Student Response: It is a red triangle.
  Teacher Comment: **To which group does it belong?**
    Student Response: It belongs to the group of triangles.
  Teacher Comment: **Draw a line from the red triangle to the group of triangles.**

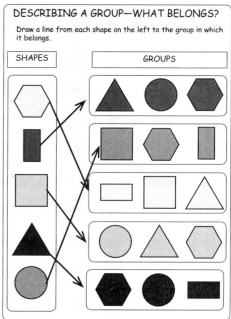

* Check students' work. Continue this dialog to discuss students' answers.

* Repeat this dialog for the items on pages 60 through 62. On page 61 students identify groups by color. On page 62 students identify groups by either shape or color.

Kindergarten Thinking Skills & Key Concepts — Teacher's Manual

Thinking About Thinking
　Teacher Comment: **What did you pay attention to in matching shapes to groups?**
　Student Response:
　　1. I named the shape and color of the first shape.
　　2. I named the group that has the same color or shape.
　　3. I checked that it fit that group.

Personal Application
　Teacher Comment: **When do you need to group things by shape, color, or size?**
　Student Response: I look for shape, color, or size when I match socks, do puzzles, or build with blocks.

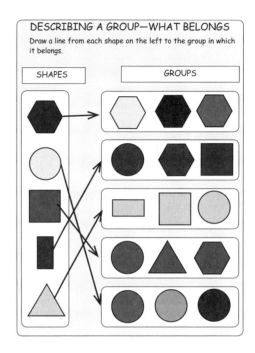

Pages 63-65 - WHICH SHAPE DOES NOT BELONG?

LESSON

Introduction
　Teacher Comment: **We have matched shapes to their groups.**

Stating the Objective
　Teacher Comment: **In this lesson you will look at a collection of shapes. You will decide how most of them are alike, and cross out the shape that does not belong to the group.**

Conducting the Lesson
　Teacher Comment: **How are most of the shapes in the example box alike?**
　　Student Response: Four of the shapes are purple.
　Teacher Comment: **Why is one shape crossed out?**
　　Student Response: The blue hexagon is not purple.
　Teacher Comment: **How are most of the next group alike?**
　　Student Response: Four shapes are squares.
　Teacher Comment: **Which one should be crossed out?**
　　Student Response: The purple rectangle is not a square and should be crossed out.
　Teacher Comment: **Now draw an "X" on the shape that does not belong to the group.**

- Check students' work. Continue this dialog to discuss students' answers.

- Repeat this process for pages 64 and 65.

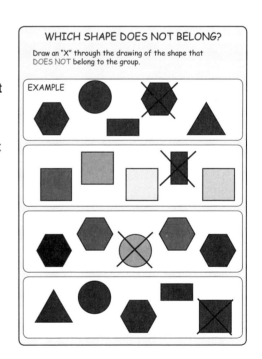

Thinking About Thinking

Teacher Comment: **What did you pay attention to in order to find the shape did not belong to the group?**

Student Response:
1. I looked to see how four of the shapes were alike.
2. I named the characteristic of the group. (Same color, or same shape.)
3. I crossed out the shape that didn't belong to the group.

Personal Application

Teacher Comment: **When do you need to find an object that does not belong to the group?**

Student Response: Sorting eating or cooking utensils; sorting construction toys or tools; sorting edge pieces from interior pieces in a picture puzzle; organizing objects or materials at home or in school.

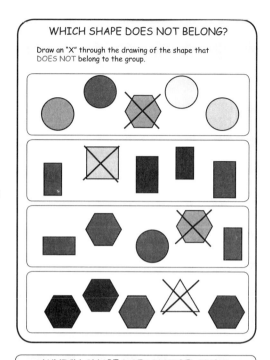

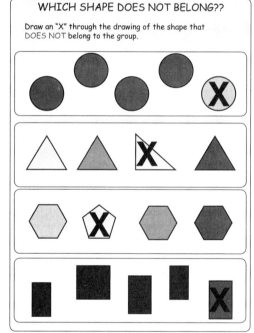

Kindergarten Thinking Skills & Key Concepts — Teacher's Manual

Pages 66-68 - SORTING SHAPES

LESSON

Introduction
Teacher Comment: **We have found how groups of shapes are alike. We have classified them by shape and color.**

Stating the Objective
Teacher Comment: **In this lesson you will sort shapes by color, size, and shape.**

Conducting the Lesson
Teacher Comment: **Notice the two boxes. One is for blue shapes. The other is for red shapes. Draw a line from each red shape to the "red shapes" box and then draw a line from each blue shape to the "blue shapes" box.**

- Check students' work. Continue this dialog to discuss students' answers.

- Repeat this dialog for pages 67 and 68

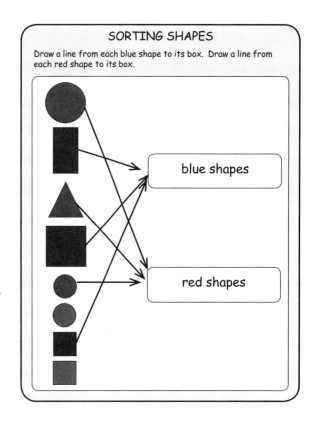

Thinking About Thinking
Teacher Comment: **What did you pay attention to in order to sort the shapes?**
Student Response:
1. I looked for shapes with the same color, the same shape, or the same kind.
2. I drew lines to the correct box.

Personal Application
Teacher Comment: **When do you need to sort objects by shape, color, or size?**
Student Response: I need to sort things by shape, color, or size when I put away spoons and forks; when I sort toys, tools, pictures, or crayons.

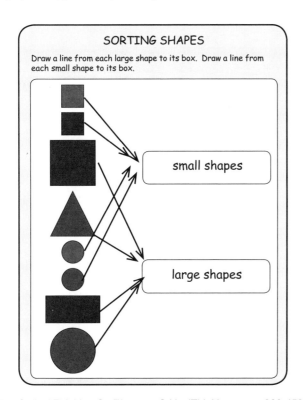
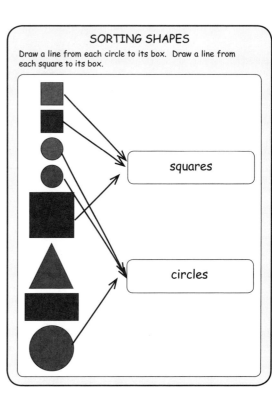

© 2015 The Critical Thinking Co.™ • www.CriticalThinking.com • 800-458-4849

CHAPTER SIX – THINKING ABOUT FAMILY MEMBERS (Pages 70-74)

TEACHING ABOUT FAMILY MEMBERS

CURRICULUM APPLICATIONS
Social Studies: Examine roles of family members and cite examples of interdependence; identify how human needs are met within the family in different cultures; examine the roles of various family members in celebrating holidays and traditions across cultures; explore the rights and responsibilities of various family members
Social Studies: Classify likenesses and differences of people; identify how a family depends upon products and services to meet its needs; cite examples of community needs and services; identify jobs within the community and understand how community helpers are an example of interdependence

LANGUAGE INTEGRATION ACTIVITIES
- Drawing: Each student may draw his or her family. Label the drawing with a description of that family member. Students' drawings may be used to create a "big book."

- Listening: Prior to a lesson that features a family member, read aloud a non-fiction picture book about that person. Language experiences with picture books extend this lesson and demonstrate how family members across cultures meet family needs. After discussing any of the picture books ask the following questions:
  Are there any new ideas about (<u>any family member</u>) that we learned from this story?
  What ideas or details about (<u>any family member</u>) did you get from the pictures?

- Storytelling: Ask students to describe to a partner a special event that his or her family enjoyed. Ask the storyteller to relate how each family member discussed in this lesson contributed to the event.

FOLLOW-UP ACTIVITIES AT HOME
- Students may take home the family tree diagram and ask parents to help them fill in the names to show family relationships. Students may draw pictures of family members in the boxes to create a family drawing, or individual drawings may be organized by the teacher into a poster-size family tree diagram.

- Encourage students to explain how family needs are met if the family member being described is not present in the home, i.e. extended families, single parent families, etc. Students may describe non-family members who fulfill the traditional roles of family members.

TEACHING SUGGESTIONS
- If any children in your class live in foster homes, conduct discussion of family members cautiously in order to avoid the distress or confusion that discussing families creates for these children.
- Young children may not commonly use the term "gender" to mean male or female or relative to mean someone in one's family. Encourage students to use these terms and to find synonyms for them.
- Students may not commonly use the term "toddler." Explain how the word was derived and the ages and capabilities that one usually associates with a toddler. Students may realize that the term "toddler," like "baby," may refer to children of either gender.
- Ask students to describe to a partner a special event that his or her family enjoyed. Ask the storyteller to relate how each family member contributed to the event.
- Students may take home the family tree diagram and ask their parents to help them fill in the names of family members or draw pictures of family members in the boxes.
- Encourage students to explain how family needs are met if the family member being described is not present in the home, i.e., extended families, single-parent families, etc. Students may describe individuals who are not family members, but fulfill traditional roles.
- For households in which children are raised by grandparents, children may call the grandparent "mother" or "father." Be aware of possible confusion as those students respond.
- In some Native American groups cousins may be called brothers. This may create some confusion about identifying grandparents for teachers unfamiliar with Native American clans and the terms assigned to family relationships.
- Teachers may use graphic organizers for bulletin board displays, student art work, or end-of-unit summary lessons. An example is shown. For a blank graphic see the appendix.

MENTAL MODEL

A mental model is a framework for understanding a concept. It outlines the characteristics that one must state to describe or define a concept. After completing this chapter, each kindergarten student will have applied this mental model to family members in the lessons. A mental model helps a student:

- Anticipate what he or she needs to know to understand a new family member
- Remember the characteristics of a family members
- State a clear definition or write an adequate description of a family member
- Explain family members to someone else

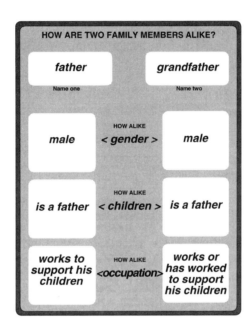

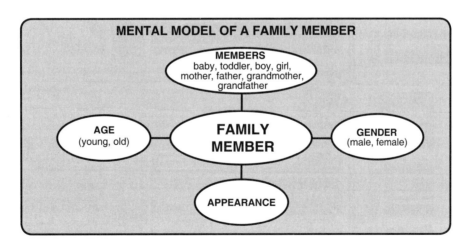

Kindergarten Thinking Skills & Key Concepts | Teacher's Manual

Page 70 - DESCRIBING FAMILY MEMBERS

LESSON

Introduction
- Without identifying whom you have chosen, describe a student to the class in three to five sentences.
    Teacher Comment: **Whom did I describe?**
       Student Response: Responses will vary.
    Teacher Comment: **What clues let you know whom I described?**
       Student Response: The person's height, coloring, behavior, what each student adds to the class, and personality.

Stating the Objective
   Teacher Comment: **I will describe a family member and then ask you to circle the picture of that family member.**

Conducting the Lesson
   Teacher Comment: **Listen to this description of a family member. This family member remembers events and places other family members don't know about. She may live nearby or far away. She is an older woman whose son or daughter is a mother or father. She helps her grandchildren know they are loved and special. She sometimes takes care of her grandchildren. Which family member did I describe?**
      Student Response: That family member is a grandmother.
   Teacher Comment: **Circle the picture of this family member.**

   Teacher Comment: **Name the family members in the other pictures.**
      Student Response: They are a mother and a girl.
   Teacher Comment: **What clues let you know that the person in the picture is a grandmother?**
      Student Response: Answers will vary. I decided which person looks older and what she does.
   Teacher Comment: **Why don't the other family members fit the description?**
      Student Response: The girl is too young to be a grandmother. The mother looks too young to have grown children.
   Teacher Comment: **Look at the second row. Listen to this description of a family member. This family member is not as tall as a sink. His mother can lift him, but he is too heavy to carry very far. He is learning to talk and walk by himself. He has some teeth and can eat many cut-up foods by himself. He knows his family and where to find things in the house. Which family member did I describe?**
      Student Response: That family member is a toddler.
   Teacher Comment: **Circle the picture of this family member.**

   Teacher Comment: **Name the family members in the other pictures.**
      Student Response: They are a baby and a boy.

- Allow students time to work and then discuss their answers.

   Teacher Comment: **What clues let you know that the person in the picture is a toddler boy?**
      Student Response: I could tell that he is a young child because of his size compared to the toy.
   Teacher Comment: **Name the family members in the other pictures. Why don't they fit the description?**
      Student Response: The baby can't talk or walk. The boy does not need someone to cut his food.
   Teacher Comment: **Look at the last row of family members. Listen to this description of a family member. This family member has friends that she shares her things with. She may know how to swim, roller skate, or ride a bicycle. She is old enough to go to school. She can read books and solve some arithmetic problems.**

   Teacher Comment: **Circle the picture of this family member.**
   Teacher Comment: **Name the family members in the other pictures.**

Teacher Comment: **What clues let you know that the person in the picture is a girl?**
Student Response: She looks older than the baby or the toddler. She has longer hair. She has books in her hands
Teacher Comment: **Name the family members in the other pictures. Why don't they fit the description?**
Student Response: The baby and toddler are too young to do any of these activities. Both are smaller than a school-age child.

Thinking About Thinking
Teacher Comment: **What did you look for to pick the family member that was described?**
Student Response:
1. I remembered the important details of the family member (the person's age, gender, relationships to other members of the family, roles, my feelings about him or her, interests or experiences that make that person special).
2. I found the important details in the pictures.
3. I checked that the other pictures of family members don't show those important details as well.

Personal Application
Teacher Comment: **When is it important to describe family members?**
Student Response: I must describe family members in order to relate incidents that happen at home, to explain how each family member helps the family meet its needs, to introduce family members to friends, to write or tell stories about family members.

Pages 71-72 - DESCRIBING FAMILY MEMBERS

LESSON

- Use the term "adult" to describe family members who are no longer children. Students may or may not use the term in their responses.

Introduction
Teacher Comment: **We have noticed whether a family member is younger or older.**
Teacher Comment: **What are the details that show whether are person is younger or older.**
Student Response: You can tell the difference by their height, appearance, and behavior.

Stating the Objective
Teacher Comment: **You will look at pictures of family members and decide whether the person is young or old.**

Conducting the Lesson
Teacher Comment: **Trace and copy the words "old" and "young."**
Teacher Comment: **You know that a baby is a young child. Notice that a line has been drawn from the picture of the baby to the word "young." Who is the family member in the next picture?**
Student Response: The next picture shows a grandmother.
Teacher Comment: **What clues let you know that the grandmother is old?**
Student Response: Her wrinkled face and white hair made me think she is old
Teacher Comment: **The grandmother is an older person. She is an adult. Draw a line from the picture of grandmother to the word "old."**
Teacher Comment: **Who is the next family member?**
Student Response: The next picture shows a grandfather.
Teacher Comment: **The grandfather is an older person. He is an adult. Draw a line from the picture of grandfather to the word that describes him.**

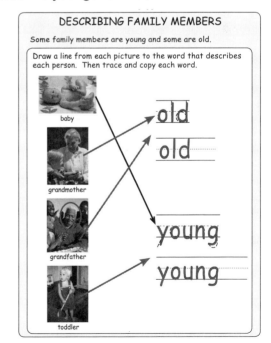

- Check students' work. Continue this dialog to discuss students' answers.

> Teacher Comment: **What clues let you know that the grandfather is old?**
> Student Response: His gray hair made me think he is old.
> Teacher Comment: **Who is the family member in the next picture?**
> Student Response: The next picture shows a toddler.
> Teacher Comment: **Draw a line from the bottom picture, toddler, to the word that describes his age.**

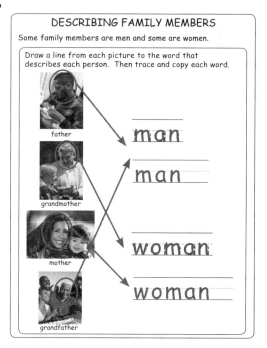

> Teacher Comment: **What clues let you know that this family member is young?**
> Student Response: The appearance and activity shows me he is young.
> Teacher Comment: **Open your books to page 72.**
> Teacher Comment: **When we use the words "boy" or "girl," "mother" or "father," or "grandmother" or "grandfather," we are describing whether they are male or female. We are describing their gender.**

> Teacher Comment: **Draw a line from each picture to the word that describes him or her.**

Thinking About Thinking
> Teacher Comment: **What did you look for to tell whether the family member was young or old?**
> Student Response: I guessed their age by their appearance. They look like people I know who are young or old.
> Teacher Comment: **How did you know if the person in the picture is a man or a woman?**
> Student Response: Their hair, faces, bodies, and clothes look like a man's or a woman's.

Personal Application
> Teacher Comment: **When is it important to know if a person is young or old?**
> Student Response: If a person is very young or very old, they may need help. I need to treat the very young with gentle care and the old with respect and politeness.

Page 73 - DESCRIBING FAMILY MEMBERS

LESSON

Introduction:
> Teacher Comment: **In the last two lessons we learned about age and gender by matching pictures to words.**

Stating the Objective
> Teacher Comment: **In this lesson you will describe family members shown in photographs, then trace and copy their names.**

Conducting the Lesson
> Teacher Comment: **Name and describe the family member pictured in the first box. Describe this family member to your partner.**
> Student Response: A baby is less than a year old and may be a boy or a girl. He or she must be dressed and fed milk or soft food. A baby may have tiny teeth or no teeth at all. He or she needs diapers. A baby learns to sit, crawl, play, smile, talk, and walk. He or she must be cared for by an adult.
> Teacher Comment: **What details do you need in order to describe or explain that the person in this picture is a baby?**
> Student Response: I looked at the picture to know his age (younger than a year old), his small size (compared to the pictures on the blanket), what his body looks like (his legs are still curved and don't look strong enough for walking), what he wears, what he can do.

Teacher Comment: **Trace and copy the word "baby."**

Teacher Comment: **Describe the next family member to your partner.**
  Student Response: This man is old enough to have children. Some fathers live in the same house as their children; others don't. A father works for money for the family. Sometimes fathers work at home. Fathers teach their children how to do things, like riding a bike, or how to behave.
Teacher Comment: **What details do you need in order to describe or explain that the person in this picture is a father?**
  Student Response: His age, his relationship to children, what he does to help children grow up healthy and safe, how he contributes to the family.
Teacher Comment: **Trace and copy the word "father."**

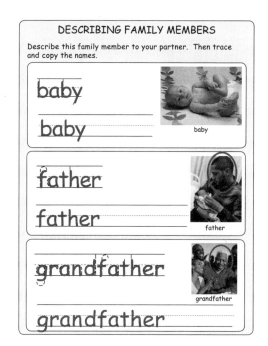

Teacher Comment: **Describe the next family member to your partner.**
  Student Response: This is an older man whose son or daughter is a father or mother. Sometimes he takes care of his grandchildren. He remembers events and places that younger members of the family don't know about. He helps his grandchildren understand that they are loved and special. Some grandfathers live nearby; others live far away.
Teacher Comment: **What details do you need in order to describe or explain that the person in this picture is a grandfather?**
  Student Response: I saw that he looks old enough to be an adult's father.
Teacher Comment: **Trace and copy the word "grandfather."**

Thinking About Thinking
  Teacher Comment: **What do you think about to describe a member of a family?**
  Student Response:
  1. I recalled the important details of the family member (the person's age, gender, relationships to other members of the family, roles, interests or experiences that make them special.)
  2. I checked that I describe all those important details.
  3. I checked that I have given enough details to keep that family member from being confused for another relative.

Personal Application
  Teacher Comment: **When is it important to describe family members well?**
  Student Response: I must describe family members to tell about something that happened at home, to explain how each family member helps the family, to introduce family members to friends, to tell or to write stories or journals about family members.

Page 74 - SIMILAR FAMILY MEMBERS

LESSON
- Emphasize the wording commonly used to describe similarities and differences. Repeat words that show similarity (both, and, like, similar, resemble, etc.) and encourage students to use them in their responses. Explain the term "unlike" and encourage students use words that cue differences (but, not, different, opposite, and unlike).

Introduction
  Teacher Comment: **We have described family members. We know that a person who is no longer a child is an adult. We say that he or she has "grown up."**

Stating the Objective
  Teacher Comment: **In this lesson we will identify a family member that is most like another one.**

Class Activity – Example:
Teacher Comment: In the example you see a picture of a grandmother. Tell your partner all the important things that you would need to say to describe a grandmother.

Teacher Comment: **What information describes a grandmother?**
Student Response: A grandmother is an older woman whose son or daughter is a father or mother. Sometimes grandmothers take care of their grandchildren. Grandmothers remember events and places that younger members of the family may not know.

Teacher Comment: **Which person has most of the same important characteristics as a grandmother?**
Student Response: A mother is a woman who has a son or daughter. Usually mothers take care of their children. Mothers help children get food, keep them clean and safe, and teach children how to take care of themselves. Like grandmothers, mothers show a child that he or she is loved and special.

Teacher Comment: **What clues let you know that a mother is most like a grandmother?**
Student Response: I thought about her age, gender, and her care of children.

Teacher Comment: **How are the father and toddler boy different from the mother and grandmother?**
Student Response: The father and the toddler boy are males, unlike the grandmother who is a female. The toddler is a child, unlike the grandmother who is an adult.

Teacher Comment: **Look at the middle exercise. What information describes a toddler?**
Student Response: Toddlers are two years old or younger. They can still be lifted and carried, but not for a long distance. They are learning to talk and walk by themselves (toddle). A toddler has some teeth and can eat many foods by themselves if it is cut into small pieces. Toddlers can recognize their family and know where to find things in their home.

Teacher Comment: **What family member has most of the same characteristics as the toddler?**
Student Response: A baby is less than a year old and may be boy or girl. He or she must be dressed and fed milk or soft food. A baby may have tiny teeth or no teeth at all. He or she needs diapers. A baby learns to sit, crawl, play, smile, talk, and walk. He or she has to be cared for by an adult.

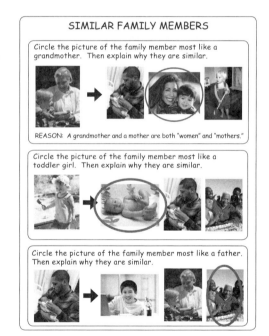

Teacher Comment: **What clues let you know that a baby is most like a toddler?**
Student Response: The toddler is small, needs to be carried, is a child.

Teacher Comment: **How are the other members unlike the toddler and baby?**
Student Response: The father and grandfather are adults much older than the baby or toddler.

- Repeat the same directions to compare a father to a grandfather.

Thinking About Thinking
Teacher Comment: **What do you think about to compare family members?**
Student Response:
1. I recalled the important details of the two family members. (Age, gender, relationships to other members of the family, roles, feelings about them, interests or experiences that make them special).
2. I looked for similar details in the other family members.
3. I selected the family member that has most of the same details.
4. I checked to see that other family members do not fit the important details better than the one I selected.

Personal Application
Teacher Comment: **When is it important to describe family members well?**
Student Response: I need to describe family members when I tell about what happens at home, to explain how each family member helps the family meet its needs, to introduce family members to friends, or to tell or write stories about family members.

CHAPTER SEVEN – THINKING ABOUT FOOD (Pages 75-86)

TEACHING ABOUT FOOD

CURRICULUM APPLICATIONS
Health: Recognize foods that provide good nutrition; identify a variety of foods
Science: Recognize examples of common animals as being fish, birds, or mammals; identify, illustrate, and describe the parts of a plant (root, stem, seed, and leaf); identify how plants are important to people; identify living things as plants or animals, recognize the major physical differences between plants and animals; identify examples of various types of foods (dairy, meat, fruit, vegetables, and grains) identify the key characteristics of different types of food (source, appearance, taste, how prepared, how eaten, and special ethnic or cultural uses)

LANGUAGE INTEGRATION ACTIVITIES
- A list of food discussed in this chapter is provided in the appendix. To help students associate the word with the picture of the food, enlarge this list for display and refer to the term for various foods as you teach the lesson.

- Drawing: Ask students to draw a picture of a food. Students may write or give short descriptions or riddles about the food. Label the drawing with a description of that food. Students' drawings may be used to create a "big book."

- Listening: Prior to a lesson that features a food, read aloud a non-fiction picture book about that food. Language experiences with picture books extend this lesson and demonstrate how food is prepared across cultures. After discussing any of the picture books ask the following questions:
  Are there any new ideas about (any food) that we learned from this story?
  What ideas or details about (any food) did you get from the pictures?
  Is this information true of most (any food)?

- Storytelling: Ask students to describe to a partner a special event at which a special food was served. Ask the storyteller to relate how the food was prepared and enjoyed.

- Select a common story or fairy tale about food, such as *The Little Red Hen*. Ask students to retell the story about another food (e.g. using butter instead of bread). Discuss how the revised story is different from the original. For example the steps in making butter will be different.

TEACHING SUGGESTIONS
- Use fresh vegetables to supplement this lesson. Whenever possible, select vegetables that are still intact with the stalks, root hairs, and leaves that are usually removed at the supermarket. For example, young children may not realize that the portion of the carrot that we eat is the root. Showing them the green tops and root hairs lets them see how the food has been changed before it gets to the customer and to understand that the root holds valuable nutrients for the plant and for the person eating it.

- If the food is a plant product, describe the type of plant that produces it (tree, vine, bush) and identify the part of the plant that we eat (seed, fruit, leaf, stem, or root). Describe the food's color, shape, and size.

- If the food is an animal product, describe the kind of animal that produces it and how it is prepared.

- Use pictures and encourage students to give examples of the same foods prepared differently in various ethnic backgrounds. Provide pictures of ethnic foods from magazines or cookbooks or provide samples of ethnic foods using food mentioned in the lesson. Assist students in describing and pronouncing the names of ethnic foods. Discuss how its preparation and combination with other foods affects its appearance and taste.

- "Beans" and "peas" are used interchangeably to describe legumes. Commonly "bean" means that one eats the whole pod, including the seed portion, such as green beans. Seeds are commonly called "peas," such as black-eyed peas or green peas. However the seed portion can be also be called beans, such as black beans, garbanzo beans, or lima beans. Trying to distinguish between beans and peas is probably not useful.

- Science texts offer the scientific definition of fruit which also applies to foods commonly called vegetables (tomatoes, squash, cucumbers, pumpkins, etc.). Clarify students' use of the term fruit in appropriate contexts: "vegetable" in cookbooks and grocery stores, "fruit" in scientific discussion of parts of a plant.

- While we describe a potato as the root part of the plant, it is actually a tuber, a short thickened portion of an underground stem. Since most adults believe that a potato is part of the root, the more accurate designation of a potato as tuber can be clarified in later grades.
- Many young children do not know how butter and cheese are made. Films and picture books may help them understand these processes.
- Teachers may use the graphic organizers (shown below and included in the appendix) to define terms or for bulletin board displays, student art work, or end-of-unit summary lessons.

  After classification exercises, students may create a group display. Each group of four students will use a large sheet of newsprint, pictures of foods, or index cards labeled with the names of various foods. Using a large branching diagram as a background, students sort the pictures or labels to create a display.

MENTAL MODEL
A mental model is a framework for understanding a concept. It outlines the characteristics that one must state to describe or define a concept. After completing this chapter, each kindergarten student will have applied this mental model to foods in the lessons. A mental model helps a student:

- Anticipate what he or she needs to know to understand a new food
- Remember the characteristics of a food
- State a clear definition or write an adequate description of a food
- Explain a food to someone else

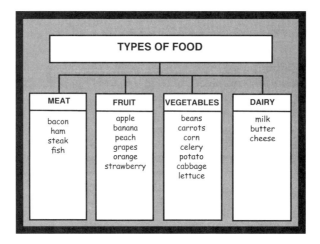

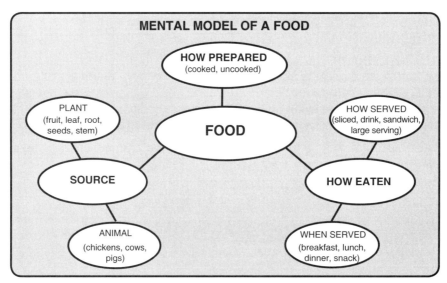

Kindergarten Thinking Skills & Key Concepts　　　　　　　　　　　　　　　　　Teacher's Manual

Page 76 - DESCRIBING FOOD

LESSON

Introduction

- Select a food and bring a sample or the package to class. Describe the food to the class.
  Teacher Comment: **What food did I describe?**
  Teacher Comment: **What clues let you know what food I was describing?**
    Student Response: The kind of food (fruit, bread, meat, drink, etc.), where one gets it, or how it is prepared.

Stating the Objective
　　Teacher Comment: **In this lesson I will describe a food and you will select it.**

Conducting the Lesson
　　Teacher Comment: **Look at the top row. Name these foods.**
　　　Student Response: The foods are bread, butter, and cheese.
　　Teacher Comment: **I will describe one of the foods. Select the picture that fits the following description. This food is made by mixing flour, water, salt, and oil or butter. This food is usually white or light brown, and is not as sweet as desserts. The bakery often slices it so that we can use it for toast or sandwiches.**

- Ask students to decide with their partners which picture has been described.
  Teacher Comment: **What do we call this food?**
    Student Response: This food is bread.
  Teacher Comment: **Circle the picture of the bread.**

  Teacher Comment: **What clues let you know that the food in this picture is bread?**
    Student Response: It looks like loaves of bread that are sliced used for sandwiches or toast (same size, shape, and color).
  Teacher Comment: **Why don't the other foods fit this description?**
    Student Response: Butter and cheese are made from milk and melt if heated.

  Teacher Comment: **Look at the second row of photographs. Name these foods.**
    Student Response: The foods are carrots, onions, and an orange.
  Teacher Comment: **Select the picture that fits the following description. This long orange vegetable can be eaten cooked or served raw. It can be sliced, chopped, or eaten whole. The part that we eat is the root of the plant. It is pulled out of the ground by grabbing the green leaves that stick up at the top.**

- Ask students to decide with their partners which picture has been described.
  Teacher Comment: **What do we call this food?**
    Student Response: This food is a carrot.
  Teacher Comment: **Circle the picture of the carrot.**

  Teacher Comment: **What clues let you know that the food in this picture is the carrot?**
    Student Response: Its orange color, and long shape show that it is a carrot.
  Teacher Comment: **Why don't the other foods fit this description?**
    Student Response: Onions are white, yellow, or purple. Oranges are fruit, not roots, and they grow on trees.

  Teacher Comment: **Select the picture that fits the following description. This food is a tight ball of leaves that grows close to the ground. It can be green or purple. It can be eaten cooked or raw.**
- Ask students to decide with their partners which picture has been described.
  Teacher Comment: **What do we call this food?**
    Student Response: This food is a cabbage.
  Teacher Comment: **Circle the picture of the cabbage.**

© 2015 The Critical Thinking Co.™ • www.CriticalThinking.com • 800-458-4849

Teacher Comment: **What clues let you know that the food in this picture is a cabbage?**
Student Response: The part of the plant that we eat and how it is prepared show that this food is cabbage.
Teacher Comment: **Why do the other foods not fit this description?**
Student Response: Beans and peas are part of the seed pod. Peas and beans are not a ball of leaves.

Thinking About Thinking
Teacher Comment: **What did you look for when you picked out the food that was described?**
Student Response:
1. I recalled the important details of the food. (What it looks like, its taste, how it's prepared, when it is usually eaten, etc.)
2. I found the important details in the pictures.
3. I checked that the pictures of other foods do not show those important details.

Personal Application
Teacher Comment: **When is it important to describe food accurately?**
Student Response: I must describe the food in the school cafeteria or in a restaurant, to remind a friend or family member about food that he or she has been asked to bring home from the grocery store, to understand or relate a doctor's diet recommendations, or to help someone who doesn't understand English well to request food that he or she wants.

Page 77 - DESCRIBING FOOD

LESSON

Introduction
Teacher Comment: **We have identified food that fits a particular description.**

Stating the Objective
Teacher Comment: **In this lesson you will describe some foods, then trace and copy their names.**

Conducting the Lesson
Teacher Comment: **Name the first food and describe it to your partner.**

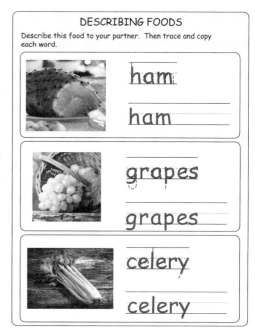

- Check that students include these details:
    Student Response: This food is ham (the meat of a pig). It is usually cooked in large pieces. We usually eat ham in sandwiches, soups, or in large pieces for dinner or breakfast.
    Teacher Comment: **Trace and copy "ham" in the lined spaces.**

    Teacher Comment: **What details do you describe to explain that the food in the picture is ham?**
    Student Response: I described the size of the pieces we cook and eat. I explained what animal the meat comes from.

    Teacher Comment: **Look at the second food on this page. Name this food and describe it to your partner.**
    Student Response: This food is grapes. It is a fruit that grows in bunches on a vine. The soft, sweet, green or purple berry can be eaten whole, made into jelly, or squeezed into juice.
    Teacher Comment: **Trace and copy "grapes" in the lined spaces.**

    Teacher Comment: **What details do you describe to explain that the food in the picture is grapes?**
    Student Response: I described the color, shape, appearance of the grapes. I explained that it is made into jelly or squeezed into juice.

Teacher Comment: **Look at the bottom food. Name this food and describe it to your partner.**
Student Response: This food is celery. It is a vegetable that has leaves and a stalk. The stalk of this plant can be cooked or eaten raw. Some people add celery to soups or stews to give it flavor. Celery is moist and crunchy to eat and can be dipped into sauces.
Teacher Comment: **Trace and copy "celery" in the lined spaces.**

Teacher Comment: **What details do you describe to explain that the food in the picture is celery?**
Student Response: I described that we eat the stem. I told that it is eaten raw or cooked.

Thinking About Thinking
Teacher Comment: **What did you say about the food to describe it?**
Student Response:
1. I recalled the important details of the food. (What it looks like, its taste, how it's prepared, when it is usually eaten, etc.)
2. I found the important details in the pictures. (I will look for or try to recall whether it is a plant or animal product, its color, shape, flavor and size, how it is prepared, when it is commonly eaten, and special ways different groups of people prepare it.)
3. I checked that the other pictures of food don't show those important details as well.

Personal Application
Teacher Comment: **When is it important to describe food accurately?**
Student Response: I describe the food when I order food in the school cafeteria or in a restaurant; or to help someone who doesn't understand English well to request food that he or she wants.

Page 78 - DESCRIBING FOOD

TEACHING SUGGESTIONS
- One page is commonly sufficient for one 20-30 minute session in order to have time for the "Thinking About Thinking" and "Personal Application" discussions. If more than one page is done in one session, conduct the "Thinking About Thinking" and "Personal Application" discussions at the end of the session, not at the end of each exercise.

LESSON

Introduction
Teacher Comment: **In the last lesson we described some foods.**

Stating the Objective
Teacher Comment: **Now you are going to match the pictures of the foods to the word for that food.**

Conducting the Lesson
Teacher Comment: **Name the food shown in the first picture.**
Student Response: The first picture shows onions.
Teacher Comment: **Trace and copy the word "onions." Draw a line from the picture of the onions to the word "onions."**

Teacher Comment: **Name the food shown in the second picture.**
Student Response: The second picture shows carrots.
Teacher Comment: **Draw a line from the picture to the word "carrots." Trace and copy the word "carrots."**

- Continue this dialog for steak and broccoli.

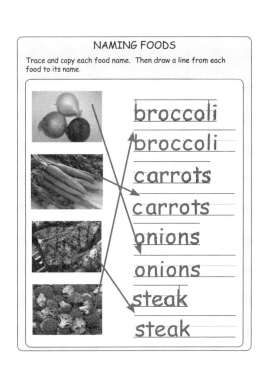

Thinking About Thinking
   Teacher Comment: **How did you decide which word belonged with each picture?**
   Student Response:
   1. I looked at the details of the food in the picture.
   2. I named that food.
   3. I found the word for that food.

Personal Application
   Teacher Comment: **When is it important to know the word for a food?**
   Student Response: I need to know the word for a food to find food in the grocery store and to order food in a restaurant.

Page 79-80 - DESCRIBING FOOD

TEACHING SUGGESTIONS
- Define dairy and grain.
  Dairy - A group of foods made from milk.
  Grain - Seeds that we eat or that are made into products we eat.

LESSON

Introduction
   Teacher Comment: **In the last lesson we named different foods.**

Stating the Objective
   Teacher Comment: **In this lesson you are going to write words that describe where various foods come from.**

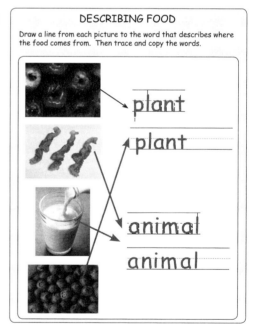

Conducting the Lesson
   Teacher Comment: **Name the food in the first picture.**
     Student Response: That food is apples.
   Teacher Comment: **Where do apples come from?**
     Student Response: Apples grow on trees. Trees are plants.
   Teacher Comment: **A line connects the picture of apple to the word "plant." Trace and copy the word "plant."**

   Teacher Comment: **Name the food in the second picture.**
     Student Response: That food is bacon.
   Teacher Comment: **Where does bacon come from?**
     Student Response: Bacon is the meat from a pig. Pigs are animals.
   Teacher Comment: **Draw a line from the picture of bacon to the word "animal." Trace and copy the word "animal."**

   Teacher Comment: **Name the food in the third picture.**
     Student Response: That food is milk.
   Teacher Comment: **Draw a line to the word that shows whether milk comes from plants or animals.**
   Teacher Comment: **In what section of the supermarket do you find milk?**
     Student Response: You find milk in the dairy section of the supermarket.

   Teacher Comment: **Name the food in the last picture.**
     Student Response: That food is blueberries.
   Teacher Comment: **Where do blueberries come from?**
     Student Response: Blueberries grow on bushes.
   Teacher Comment: **Draw a line to the word that shows whether blueberries come from plants or animals.**

- Check students' work. Continue this dialog to discuss students' answers.

Teacher Comment: **If we don't have to cook food, we can eat it raw. On page 80 you will draw a line from each picture to the word that describe whether we eat the food cooked or raw.**

Teacher Comment: **Name the food in the first picture.**
   Student Response: That food is corn.
Teacher Comment: **Do we eat corn cooked or raw?**
   Student Response: We cook corn.
   Teacher Comment: **Draw a line from the picture of corn to the word "cooked." Trace and copy the word "cooked."**

Teacher Comment: **Name the food in the second picture.**
   Student Response: That food is grapes.
Teacher Comment: **Do we eat grapes cooked or raw?**
   Student Response: We eat grapes raw.
 Teacher Comment: **Draw a line from the picture of grapes to "raw." Trace and copy the word "raw."**

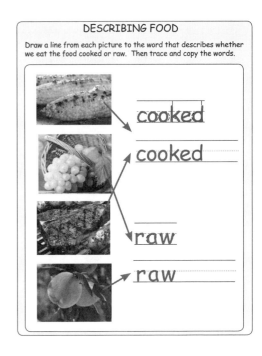

Teacher Comment: **Name the food in the third picture.**
   Student Response: The third picture is steak.
Teacher Comment: **Draw a line from the picture of steak to the word that shows whether we eat steak cooked or raw.**

Teacher Comment: **Name the food in the last picture.**
   Student Response: The last picture is a peach.
Teacher Comment: **Draw a line from the picture of peach to the word that shows whether we eat a peach cooked or raw.**

Thinking About Thinking
   Teacher Comment: **What did you say about the food to describe it?**
   Student Response:
     1. I remembered whether it comes from a plant or an animal and whether we eat it cooked or raw.
     2. I found the word to describe where it comes from or how we eat it.

Personal Application
   Teacher Comment: **When is it important to describe where food comes from or whether it is cooked?**
     Student Response: I need to describe the food when I ask for food in the school cafeteria or in a restaurant.

Pages 81-82 - DESCRIBING PARTS OF A WHOLE

Introduction
Teacher Comment: **You have learned about bread, ham, and cheese. They can be put together to make another food: a sandwich. Trace the word "sandwich."**

Teacher Comment: **Name the parts of the sandwich.**

Student Response: The parts are bread, meat, and cheese.
Teacher Comment: **What would happen if one of the parts was missing?**
Student Response: If you do not have bread, you cannot hold the sandwich. If you have bread, but no ham, you can only make a cheese sandwich. If you have bread, but no cheese, you can only make a ham sandwich.

Stating the Objective
Teacher Comment: **On page 82, like you explained the parts of a sandwich, you will explain the parts of a tree, what that part does, and what would happen to the tree if that part were missing.**

Conducting the Lesson
Teacher Comment: **What are the small, green parts of the tree that make food for the tree?**
Student Response: The green leaves make food for the tree.
Teacher Comment: **Write the word "leaves" on the top blank.**

Teacher Comment: **What would happen if the leaves were missing?**
Student Response: The tree would not have the food it needs to grow.

Teacher Comment: **What are the small, round, soft parts of the tree that hold the seeds?**
Student Response: The round parts are fruit.
Teacher Comment: **Write the word "fruit" on the second blank.**

Teacher Comment: **What would happen if the fruit was missing?**
Student Response: The tree would not be able to make the seeds needed to make more trees.

• Repeat these questions for "trunk" and "root."

Teacher Comment: **What part of the plant do we eat?**
Student Response: We eat the fruit of the plant.
Teacher Comment: **Why can't we eat the other parts of the plant?**
Student Response: The trunk and the roots are too hard to chew. Our bodies cannot use the leaves.

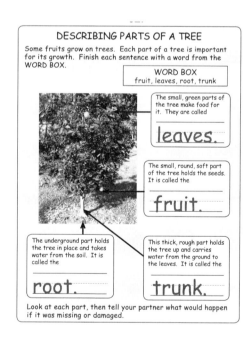

Thinking About Thinking
Teacher Comment: **What did you think about to know what part of the plant to eat?**
Student Response:
1. I named each part of the tree.
2. I thought about what each part does for the plant.
3. I looked for a part that could be food.
4. I checked why the other parts could not be food.

Personal Application

Teacher Comment: **Why is it important to know what the parts of a plant do?**
Student Response: I need to know how each part of the plant helps the plant grow.

Teacher Comment: **When should you know what part of the plant you eat?**

Student Response: I should know the parts of the plant we eat to know which parts I should not eat.

Page 83 - SIMILAR FOODS

TEACHING SUGGESTIONS

- Emphasize the wording commonly used to describe similarities and differences. Repeat words that show similarity (both, and, like, similar, resemble, etc.) and encourage students to use them in their responses. Explain the term "unlike" and encourage students use words that cue differences (but, not, different, opposite, and unlike).

- In their discussions students should include identifying the part of the plant we eat, as well as words that describe the color, taste, size, and preparation of the food.

LESSON

- To reinforce students' responses you may draw a HOW ARE THINGS ALIKE diagram to record their answers. For an example see right. For a blank graphic organizer, see the appendix.

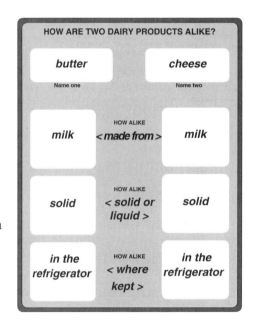

Introduction
Teacher Comment: **We have described foods and where they come from.**

Stating the Objective
Teacher Comment: **In this lesson you will identify a food that is similar to another one.**

Conducting the Lesson
Teacher Comment: **Name the foods in the example.**
Student Response: The foods are apples, carrots, onions, and an orange.
Teacher Comment: **Select the food that is most like apples. Tell your partner all the important things that you know about an apple.**
Student Response: Apples are a fruit that grows on trees. They taste sweet and are made into juice and jelly. We eat the soft part of the fruit, but not the core or the seeds. Apples have a thin red or green peel that we usually eat along with the fruit.
Teacher Comment: **Which food on the right is most like the apple?**
Student Response: An orange is most like an apple.
Teacher Comment: **What clues let you know that an orange is most like the apple?**
Student Response: Both fruits grow on trees, taste sweet, and are made into juice and jelly. We eat the soft part of the fruit, but not the seeds.
Teacher Comment: **How are the other foods different from apples?**
Student Response: Carrots and onions are both root vegetables. They are not very sweet and do not contain seeds.

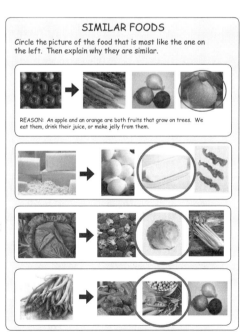

Teacher Comment: **Name the foods shown in the second row.**
Student Response: The foods are cheese, eggs, butter, and bacon.
Teacher Comment: **Tell your partner the important things you know about cheese.**
Student Response: Cheese is a food that is made from milk. It must be stored in the refrigerator and is found in the dairy section at the supermarket. It will melt at high temperatures and is used to add flavor to sandwiches or vegetables. It is good for building strong bones and teeth.
Teacher Comment: **Which food is most like cheese?**
Student Response: Butter is most like cheese.
Teacher Comment: **What clues let you know that butter is most like cheese?**
Student Response: Both are solid food that are made from milk. They have a similar color and both melt at high temperatures. Both are stored in the refrigerator at home and in the supermarket.
Teacher Comment: **How are the other foods different from cheese?**
Student Response: Bacon is made from the meat of a pig and is not a dairy product. Eggs come from chickens and are also not a dairy product.

Teacher Comment: **Name the foods shown in the third row.**
Student Response: The foods are cabbage, broccoli, lettuce, and celery.
Teacher Comment: **Tell your partner the important things you know about cabbage.**
Student Response: Cabbage is a green or purple vegetable. We eat the leaves of this plant cooked or raw. It grows as a ball of tightly wrapped leaves on small plants close to the ground.
Teacher Comment: **Which food is most like cabbage?**
Student Response: Lettuce is most like cabbage. Lettuce and cabbage are both green vegetables. We eat the leaves of these foods. Both are balls of tightly wrapped leaves that grow on small plants close to the ground. Both can be eaten raw.
Teacher Comment: **What clues let you know that the lettuce is most like cabbage?**
Student Response: Both vegetables are green, and grow as balls of leaves that grow on small plants close to the ground.
Teacher Comment: **How are the other foods different from cabbage?**
Student Response: We eat the tops of broccoli (the flowers) and the stem or stalk of celery.

Teacher Comment: **Name the foods in the last row.**
Student Response: The foods are beans, potatoes, peas, and onions.
Teacher Comment: **Tell your partner the important things you know about beans.**
Student Response: These beans are small, green vegetables that grow in pods on vines. They must be cooked. There are many different types of beans: green, yellow, kidney, lima, black, etc.
Teacher Comment: **Which food is most like beans?**
Student Response: Peas are most like beans.
Teacher Comment: **What clues let you know that beans are most like the peas?**
Student Response: Both are small, round seeds, grow on vines, and are eaten as cooked or raw vegetables.
Teacher Comment: **How are the other foods different from beans?**
Student Response: Potatoes and onions grow underground, not on vines.

Thinking About Thinking
Teacher Comment: **How do you decide which foods are most alike?**
Student Response:
1. I recalled the important details of the first food (whether the food is a plant or animal product, how it is prepared, its taste, its appearance, etc.).
2. I looked for similar details in the other foods.
3. I selected the food that has most of the same details.
4. I checked to see that other foods do not fit the important details better than the one I selected.

Personal Application
Teacher Comment: **When is it important to understand how different foods are alike?**
Student Response: I need to understand how foods are similar to explain a particular food to someone who is unfamiliar with it or to find a food to substitute for another one.

Page 84 - SIMILAR FOODS

TEACHING SUGGESTIONS
- Emphasize the wording commonly used to describe similarities. Repeat words that show similarity (both, and, like, similar, resemble, etc.) and encourage students to use them in their responses.
- To reinforce students' responses you may draw a HOW ARE THINGS ALIKE diagram to record their answers. For an example see right. For a blank graphic organizer, see the appendix.

LESSON

Introduction
  Teacher Comment: **We have selected a food that is similar to another one.**

Stating the Objective
  Teacher Comment: **In this lesson you will explain how strawberries and blueberries are alike.**

Conducting the Lesson
  Teacher Comment: **Look at the two foods in the first row. Explain how these foods are alike.**
    Student Response: Both are berries. They are small and sweet. We can eat them raw or cooked and they can be made into jam, jelly, or juice.
  Teacher Comment: **Trace and copy the words "strawberries" and "blueberries."**

  Teacher Comment: **Explain how ham and bacon are alike.**
    Student Response: Both are meat from pigs that has been processed to prevent spoilage and to give it a different flavor. Both must be cooked. Both may be broiled, fried or cooked in a microwave oven. Both may be added to soup or in a sandwich. Both may be eaten for breakfast, lunch or dinner.
  Teacher Comment: **Trace and copy the words "ham" and "bacon."**

  Teacher Comment: **Explain how beans and peas are alike.**
    Student Response: I remember that both are seeds that grow in pads on vines and are eaten as vegetables in salad or soups. Both are small and either round or oval in shape. There are many different types of beans: green, yellow, kidney, lima, black, etc. Peas are small and round.
  Teacher Comment: **Trace and copy the words "beans" and "peas."**

  Teacher Comment: **Explain how an apple and a peach are alike.**
    Student Response: Both are fruit that grow on trees.

Thinking About Thinking
  Teacher Comment: **What did you explain about food to tell how they are alike?**
    Student Response:
    1. I explained whether the food is a plant or animal product, how it is prepared, its taste, its appearance, etc.).
    2. I explained details that both foods have.
    3. I checked that I have explained the important details of both foods.

Personal Application
  Teacher Comment: **When is it important to understand how different foods are alike?**
    Student Response: I need to know how foods are alike to recognize foods that are similar to ones I already enjoy; to explain a particular food to someone.

Page 85 - KINDS OF FOOD

TEACHING SUGGESTIONS
- Each exercise is sufficient for one session in kindergarten classes, perhaps two exercises in first grade. Remember to discuss the Thinking About Thinking and Personal Application at the end of each session.
- Use the terms "groups," "types," "kind of," and "classes" to help students conceptualize classification. Encourage students to use these words in their discussions.
- Define dairy and grain:
  Dairy - the name given to a group of foods made from milk.
  Grain - Hard, dry seeds that we eat or grind up to make other products.
- This lesson is the first step in stating definitions. When forming definitions students should become accustomed to stating the category to which a person, an organism, or object belongs, as well as the distinguishing characteristics that make it different from other things of that type.

LESSON

Introduction
Teacher Comment: **We have described foods, where they come from, and whether they need to be cooked.**

Stating the Objective
Teacher Comment: **In this lesson you will match foods to their group.**

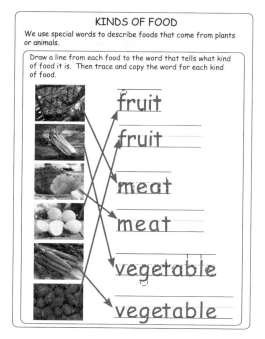

Conducting the Lesson
Teacher Comment: **What is the food in the first picture?**
Student Response: That food is steak.
Teacher Comment: **Is steak a fruit, meat, or vegetable?**
Student Response: Steak is meat.
Teacher Comment: **Draw an arrow from the picture of the steak to its class (meat). Trace and copy the word "meat."**
Teacher Comment: **What is the food in the second picture?**
Student Response: That food is celery.
Teacher Comment: **What kind of food is celery?**
Student Response: Celery is a vegetable.
Teacher Comment: **Draw an arrow from the picture of the celery to the word "vegetable." Trace and copy the word "vegetable."**

- Repeat these directions to discuss ham, lemons, carrots, and strawberries.

Thinking About Thinking
Teacher Comment: **What did you think about to decide what kind of food is shown in the picture?**
Student Response:
1. I looked at each picture and identified the food.
2. I remembered the important details about that food (whether it came from a plant or an animal, how it's prepared and where I find it in the supermarket).
3. I looked for the word for that kind of food.

Personal Application
Teacher Comment: **When is it important to know kinds of foods?**
Student Response: I need to know kinds of foods to find them in grocery stores and to select foods from menus.

Kindergarten Thinking Skills & Key Concepts   Teacher's Manual

Page 86 - KINDS OF FOOD

LESSON

Introduction
   Teacher Comment: We have learned about different kinds of food.

Stating the Objective
   Teacher Comment: **In this lesson you will find the food that does not belong with the other three foods. Remember that dairy products are foods made from milk.**

Conducting the Lesson
   Teacher Comment: **In which group do three of these foods belong?**
      Student Response: Three of the foods are dairy foods.
   Teacher Comment: **Trace the words "dairy products."**
   Teacher Comment: **Which of the foods is not a dairy product?**
      Student Response: The bacon is a meat, not a dairy product.
   Teacher Comment: **Mark out the picture of bacon.**

   Teacher Comment: **Now look at the next box. In which group do three of these foods belong?**
      Student Response: Three of the foods are green vegetables.
   Teacher Comment: **Trace the words "green vegetables."**
   Teacher Comment: **Which of the foods is not a green vegetable?**
      Student Response: The carrot is not green, it is orange.
   Teacher Comment: **Mark out the picture of the carrots.**

   Teacher Comment: **Look at the next box. In which group do three of these foods belong?**
      Student Response: Three of the foods are fruit.
   Teacher Comment: **Trace the word "fruit."**
   Teacher Comment: **Which of the foods is not a fruit?**
      Student Response: Potatoes are a vegetable, not a fruit.
   Teacher Comment: **Mark out the picture of potatoes.**

Thinking About Thinking
   Teacher Comment: **What did you think about to find the food that didn't belong?**
      Student Response:
      1. I looked at the foods and thought about what three of them had in common.
      2. I looked for the food that was different.

Personal Application
   Teacher Comment: **When is it important to know kinds of foods?**
      Student Response: I need to know kinds of foods to find them in grocery stores and to select foods from menus.

CHAPTER EIGHT – THINKING ABOUT ANIMALS (Pages 88-104)

TEACHING ABOUT ANIMALS

CURRICULUM APPLICATIONS
Science: Identify living things as plants or animals; state what animals need to live and grow; recognize examples of common animals (fish, birds, amphibians, reptiles, mammals); identify key characteristics of common types of animals (appearance, habitat, food, and locomotion)

LANGUAGE INTEGRATION ACTIVITIES

- A list of animals discussed in this chapter is provided in the appendix. To help students associate the word with the picture of the animal, enlarge this list for display and refer to the term for various animals as you teach the lesson.

- Read *What Animal Am I? An Animal Guessing Game*, by Iza Trapani (Whispering Coyote Press, Danvers, MA, 1992). This book models animal riddles with pictures. Select a picture of an animal or allow students to find or draw a picture of an animal. Ask students to create a riddle that they will tell or write for a partner.

- Drama: Ask students to use animal puppets to act out *Brown Bear, Brown Bear, What Do You See?* by Eric Carle and Bill Martin for various animals discussed in the lesson.

- Listening: Prior to a lesson that features an animal, read aloud a non-fiction picture book about that animal. Language experiences with picture books extend this lesson. After discussing any of the picture books, ask the following questions:
  Are there any new ideas about (any animal) that we learned from this story?
  What ideas or details about (any animal) did you learn from the pictures?

- Storytelling: Ask students to tell their partner a story about an animal. Ask the storyteller to relate details about the animal (appearance, habitat, food, etc.).

- Select a common story or fairy tale about an animal, such as *Are You My Mother?* by P.D. Eastman. Ask students to retell the story about another type of animal (e.g. substituting a duck and a duckling for mother bird and a baby bird). Discuss how the revised story is different from the original. For example since the duckling's home is in the water, he would meet different animals and must get home another way.

TEACHING SUGGESTIONS
- For young children "cold-blooded" or "warm-blooded" may be new terms. Explain the effect that this difference makes in the survival needs of animals.
- Create a chart or bulletin board display of different kinds of animals. Discuss how each animal reproduces, whether it is warm- or cold-blooded, and other special characteristics:
  1. Birds: egg-laying, warm-blooded animals with wings.
  2. Fish: egg-laying, cold-blooded animals with gills.
  3. Reptiles: egg-laying, cold-blooded animals with dry skin.
  4. Amphibians: egg-laying, cold-blooded animals with moist skin.
  5. Mammals: baby grows inside mother's body; warm-blooded animals with hair.

MENTAL MODEL

A mental model is a framework for understanding a concept. It outlines the characteristics that one must state to describe or define a concept. After completing this chapter, each kindergarten student will have applied this mental model to animals in the lessons. A mental model helps a student:

- Anticipate what he or she needs to know to understand a new animal
- Remember the characteristics of an animal
- State a clear definition or write an adequate description of an animal
- Explain an animal to someone else

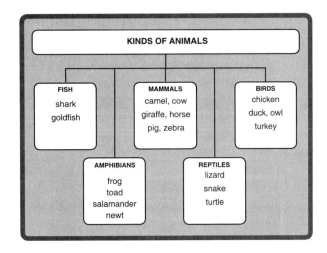

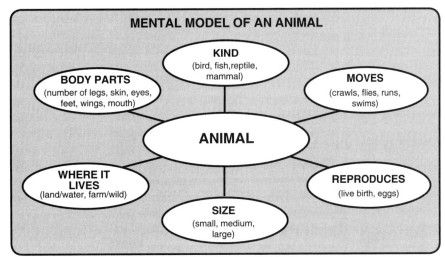

Page 88 - DESCRIBING ANIMALS

LESSON

Introduction
- In three to five sentences describe an animal that the class has studied or seen recently.

    Teacher Comment: **What animal did I describe?**
    Student Response: Responses will vary.
    Teacher Comment: **What clues let you know the animal that I described?**
    Student Response: I listened for what it looks like, coloring, behavior, how it moves, where it lives, what it eats or what animals eat it.

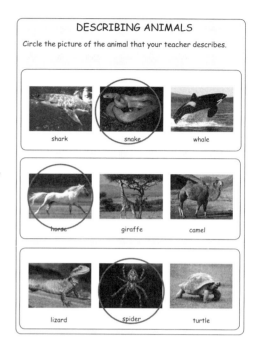

Stating the Objective
Teacher Comment: **In this lesson I will describe an animal and you will select the picture that fits this description.**

Conducting the Lesson
Teacher Comment: **Look at the top row. Name these animals.**
   Student Response: The animals are a shark, a snake, and a whale.
Teacher Comment: **Listen to the clues and then name the animal I describe. This long, thin animal slithers along the ground. It makes its home in tunnels in the ground or in dead trees. Many of them have bright colors. Some of these animals have a bite that harms people or other animals. People are often afraid of them.**
- Ask students to decide with their partners which picture has been described. Confirm the answer with the whole class. Encourage students to use as many verbs as possible to describe how the snake moves.
Teacher Comment: **Circle the picture of the snake.**

Teacher Comment: **What clues let you know that the animal in this picture is a snake?**
   Student Response: I saw its shape, how it moves, and remembered that people are often afraid of them.
Teacher Comment: **Why don't the other animals fit the description?**
   Student Response: A shark and a whale live in the ocean.

Teacher Comment: **Look at the second row. Name these animals.**
   Student Response: The animals are a horse, a giraffe, and a camel.
Teacher Comment: **Listen to the clues and then name the animal I describe. This large animal has four legs and a long tail. The long hair on its head is called a mane. It eats grass and hay. It lives on farms. People can ride on it. What do we call this animal?**
   Student Response: That animal is a horse.
Teacher Comment: **Circle the picture of the horse.**

Teacher Comment: **What clues let you know that the animal in this picture is a horse?**
   Student Response: I saw its four legs, its long tail, its mane and remembered that it lives on farms and people ride it.
Teacher Comment: **Why don't the other animals fit the description?**
   Student Response: Camels have a hump on their back and no mane. Camels are not farm animals. Giraffes have a very long neck. They don't have a long mane and are not farm animals.

Teacher Comment: **Look at the bottom row. Name these animals.**
   Student Response: The animals are a lizard, a spider, and a turtle.
Teacher Comment: **Listen to the clues and then name the animal I describe. This animal has eight legs. Its body looks like several parts which are connected. Its babies hatch from tiny eggs. This animal makes a web out of a thin thread that it makes from its body The webs become their home and a trap for flies and other insects that they eat. What do we call this animal?**

Kindergarten Thinking Skills & Key Concepts — Teacher's Manual

Student Response: This animal is a spider.
Teacher Comment: **Circle the picture of the spider.**

Teacher Comment: **What clues let you know that the animal I described is the spider?**
Student Response: The number of legs, appearance, its web, and what it eats show that it is the spider.
Teacher Comment: **Why don't the other animals fit the description?**
Student Response: Lizards and turtles have four legs. Neither lizards nor turtles spin webs.

Thinking About Thinking
Teacher Comment: **What did you look for to pick out the animal that was described?**
Student Response:
1. I recalled the important details of the animal (its appearance, color, size, whether it hatches or gives live birth, and where it lives.)
2. I found the important details in the pictures.
3. I checked that the pictures of other animals do not show those important details.

Personal Application
Teacher Comment: **When is it important to describe animals well?**
Student Response: I must describe animals on trips to the zoo, to tell about television shows, books, and pictures.

Page 89 - DESCRIBING ANIMALS

LESSON

Introduction
- Ask a student to describe to the class in three to five sentences an animal that they have studied or seen recently.
- Ask the class to name the animal that has been described.
  Teacher Comment: **What details let you know which animal was described?**
  Student Response: I listened for appearance, coloring, behavior, how it moves, where it lives, what it eats or what animals eat it.

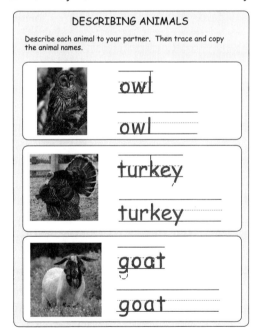

Stating the Objective
Teacher Comment: **In this lesson you will describe animals.**

Conducting the lesson
Teacher Comment: **Name the first animal and describe it to your partner.**
Student Response: The owl is a large bird that eats small animals. It has very good eyes. It comes out at night.
Teacher Comment: **Trace and write the word "owl" in the lined spaces.**

Teacher Comment: **What details do you describe to explain that the animal in the picture is an owl?**
Student Response: I described its size, what it eats, its shape and body features.

Teacher Comment: **Look at the second picture. Name this animal and describe it to your partner.**
Student Response: This animal is a turkey. A turkey is a large bird with a bare head and neck. It looks like a chicken, but is bigger. It lays eggs. Many people in the United States eat turkey for Thanksgiving dinner.
Teacher Comment: **Trace and write the word "turkey" in the lined spaces.**

Teacher Comment: **What details do you describe to explain that the animal in the picture is a turkey?**
Student Response: I described its size, shape, and when it is eaten.

Teacher Comment: **Look at the third picture. Name this animal and describe it to your partner.**
  Student Response: This animal is a goat. Goat milk is used to make goat cheese. Goats are smaller than cows. It eats grass and leaves. Goats live on farms. The baby goats look like their parents.
Teacher Comment: **Trace and write "goat" in the lined spaces.**

Teacher Comment: **What details do you describe to explain that the animal in the picture is a goat?**
  Student Response: I described its size, what it eats, and where it lives.

Thinking About Thinking
  Teacher Comment: **What do you say to describe an animal?**
  Student Response:
  1. I remembered what it looks like, whether it hatches or gives live birth, where it lives, and what it eats.
  2. I checked that I described all the important details.
  3. I checked that I told enough details to keep the animal that I am describing from being confused with another animal.

Personal Application
  Teacher Comment: **When is it important to describe animals well?**
  Student Response: I describe animals to tell about trips to the zoo, television shows, books, and pictures.

Pages 90-91 - DESCRIBING ANIMALS

TEACHING SUGGESTIONS
- One page is commonly sufficient for one 20-30 minute session in order to have time for the "Thinking About Thinking" and "Personal Application" discussions. If more than one page is done in one session, conduct the "Thinking About Thinking" and "Personal Application" discussions at the end of the session, not at the end of each exercise.

LESSON

Introduction
  Teacher Comment: **In the last lesson we described animals.**

Stating the Objective
  Teacher Comment: **In this lesson you will match a picture of an animal to its name.**

Conducting the Lesson
  Teacher Comment: **Name the animal in the first picture.**
    Student Response: That animal is a duck.
  Teacher Comment: **What details show that the animal in the picture is a duck?**
    Student Response: It is a bird that swims in lakes or rivers.
  Teacher Comment: **Notice the arrow from the picture of the duck to the word "duck." Trace and copy the word "duck."**

  Teacher Comment: **Name the second animal.**
    Student Response: That animal is a goldfish.
  Teacher Comment: **What details show that the animal in the picture is a goldfish?**
    Student Response: It is small gold or orange fish.
  Teacher Comment: **Find "goldfish" in the list of words and draw a line from the picture to the name.**
  Teacher Comment: **Trace and copy the word "goldfish."**

  Teacher Comment: **Name the animal in the third picture.**
    Student Response: That animal is a zebra.

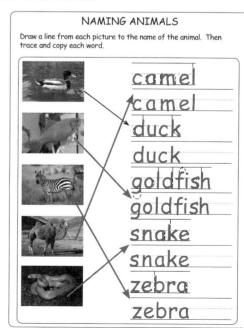

Teacher Comment: **What details show that the animal in the picture is a zebra?**
Student Response: It looks like a horse with black and white stripes.
Teacher Comment: **Find "zebra" in the list of words and draw a line from the picture to the name.**
Teacher Comment: **Trace and copy the word "zebra."**

- Repeat the same directions for camel and snake.
- On page 91 repeat the same directions for ostrich, giraffe, turtle, and shark.

Thinking About Thinking
Teacher Comment: **How did you decide which word matched each picture?**
Student Response:
1. I looked at the details of the animal in the picture.
2. I named that animal.
3. I found the word for that animal.

Personal Application
Teacher Comment: **When is it important to know the names of animals?**
Student Response: I need to know the names of animals to describe trips to the zoo, television shows, books, or pictures.

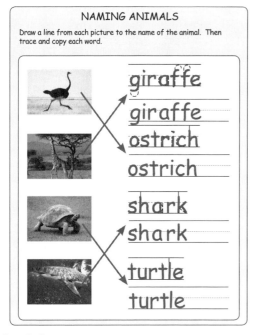

Pages 92 - DESCRIBING ANIMALS

LESSON

Introduction
Teacher Comment: **Sometimes we describe animals by their body covering. Birds have light, thin, soft feathers that can become loose or tight to keep the bird cool or warm.**
Some animals have hair – a long, thin thread that grows out of its skin. Some animals have lots of hair that becomes thick fur, like a kitten's. Its fur helps an animal stay warm or cool. On some animals there is little hair that is so thin that the skin shows through, like a human arm.
Some animals have scales – small, thin, hard pieces of skin that move slightly to allow the animal to move easily. Its body covering protects an animal from injury.

Stating the Objective
Teacher Comment: **In this lesson you will look at a picture of an animal and then decide its body covering.**

Conducting the Lesson
Teacher Comment: **Name the animal in the first picture.**
Student Response: The first picture shows a chicken.
Teacher Comment: **What is the body covering of a chicken?**
Student Response: A chicken is covered with feathers.
Teacher Comment: **Trace and copy the word "feathers." Draw a line from the picture of the chicken to the word "feathers."**

Teacher Comment: **Name the animal in the second picture.**
Student Response: The second picture shows a camel.
Teacher Comment: **What is the body covering of a camel?**
Student Response: A camel is covered with hair.
Teacher Comment: **Trace and copy the word "hair." Draw a line from the picture of the camel to the word "hair."**

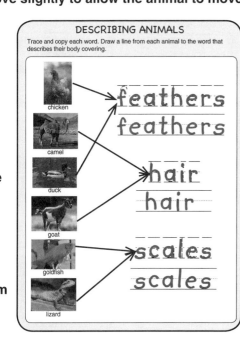

Teacher Comment: **Name the animal in the third picture.**
Student Response: The third picture shows a duck.
Teacher Comment: **What is the body covering of a duck?**
Student Response: A duck is covered with feathers.
Teacher Comment: **Draw a line from the picture of the duck to the word "feathers."**

Teacher Comment: **Name the animal in the fourth picture.**
Student Response: The fourth picture shows a goat.
Teacher Comment: **What is the body covering of a goat?**
Student Response: A goat is covered with hair.
Teacher Comment: **Draw a line from the picture of the goat to the word "hair."**

Teacher Comment: **Name the animal in the fifth picture.**
Student Response: The fifth picture shows a goldfish.
Teacher Comment: **What is the body covering of a goldfish?**
Student Response: A goldfish is covered with scales.
Teacher Comment: **Trace and copy the word "scales." Draw a line from the picture of the goldfish to the word "scales."**

Teacher Comment: **Name the animal in the bottom picture.**
Student Response: The bottom picture shows a lizard.
Teacher Comment: **What is the body covering of a lizard?**
Student Response: A lizard is covered with scales.
Teacher Comment: **Draw a line from the picture of the lizard to the word "scales."**

- Extend this lesson by asking the student to name other animals that have feathers, hair, or scales. Confirm that students understand that an animal's body covering keeps it warm or cool and protects the body from injury. Students should recognize the significance of body covering in identifying various animals.

Thinking About Thinking
Teacher Comment: **What did you look for to describe the body covering of various animals?**
Student Response:
1. I looked at each picture and identified the animal.
2. I looked at the details to see what its body covering is made of (feathers, hair, or scales).
3. I looked for the word that describes the animal's body covering.

Personal Application
Teacher Comment: **When is it important to describe an animal's body covering?**
Student Response: I need to describe an animal's body covering to explain what kind of animal it is and to understand how an animal stays warm or cool and how its body covering protects it from injury.

Pages 93 - DESCRIBING ANIMALS

Introduction
  Teacher Comment: **Sometimes we describe animals by telling how they move. Some animals have long legs that help them hop or run fast. Some animals have short legs and crawl slowly. Some animals have fins. Fins are small, thin, hard, moving parts on the back, sides, bottom, or tail of a fish that helps it move easily and quickly through water. Some animals have thin, flat, wide wings that help them fly quickly through the air.**

Stating the Objective
  Teacher Comment: **In this exercise you will draw a line from each picture to the word that describes how that animal moves.**
  Teacher Comment: **Name the animal in the first picture.**
     Student Response: The first picture shows a horse.
  Teacher Comment: **How does the horse move?**
     Student Response: The horse has long legs and runs fast.
  Teacher Comment: **Draw a line from the picture of the horse to the word "runs." Trace and copy the word "runs."**

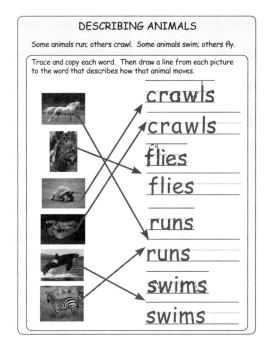

  Teacher Comment: **Name the animal in the second picture.**
     Student Response: The second animal is an owl.
  Teacher Comment: **How does the owl move?**
     Student Response: The owl has wings and flies through the air.
  Teacher Comment: **Draw a line from the picture of the owl to the word "flies." Trace and copy the word "flies."**

  Teacher Comment: **Name the animal in the third picture.**
     Student Response: The third animal is a turtle.
  Teacher Comment: **How does the turtle move?**
     Student Response: The turtle has short legs and crawls along the ground.
  Teacher Comment: **Draw a line from the picture of the turtle to the word "crawls." Trace and copy the word "crawls."**

  Teacher Comment: **Name the animal in the fourth picture.**
     Student Response: The fourth animal is a snake.
  Teacher Comment: **How does the snake move?**
     Student Response: The snake has no legs and crawls along the ground.
  Teacher Comment: **Draw a line from the picture of the snake to the word "crawls."**

  Teacher Comment: **Name the animal in the fifth picture.**
     Student Response: The fifth animal is a whale.
  Teacher Comment: **How does the whale move?**
     Student Response: The whale has fins and swims through the water.
  Teacher Comment: **Draw a line from the picture of the whale to the word "swims." Trace and copy the word "swims."**

- Continue this dialog for zebra.
  - Extend this lesson by asking the student to name other animals that crawl, fly, run, or swim. Students should name the body part that makes the animal move. Students should relate how an animal moves through its habitat (land, air, or water). Confirm that students understand that an animal's ability to move quickly protects it from injury by animals that could harm it. Students should recognize that animals must move in search of food.

Thinking About Thinking
    Teacher Comment: **What did you look for to describe how an animal moves?**
    Student Response:
    1. I looked at each picture and identified the animal.
    2. I looked at the details to see what body part makes it move and whether it moves on land, through the air, or in water.
    3. I looked for the word that describes how the animal moves.

Personal Application
    Teacher Comment: **When is it important to describe how an animal moves?**
    Student Response: I need to describe how an animal moves to explain what kind of animal it is, to tell how its body parts (legs, wings, or fins) help it move quickly or slowly, to understand how it moves across land, through the air, or in the water, and to explain how its movement helps it find food and protects it from injury.

Page 94 – DESCRIBING ANIMALS

LESSON

Introduction
    Teacher Comment: **We describe animals as small, medium, or large by comparing their size to other animals of the same kind.**

Stating the Objective
    Teacher Comment: **In this lesson you will describe the size of animals as small, medium, or large.**

Conducting the Lesson
    Teacher Comment: **Name the animals in the first box.**
        Student Response: The animals are a duck, an ostrich, and a turkey.
    Teacher Comment: **What kind of animals are these?**
        Student Response: These animals are birds.
    Teacher Comment: **The pictures make the animals look like they are the same size. Look at the surroundings and what you know about the animals to decide its size compared to the others.**
    Teacher Comment: **Which animal is the smallest?**
        Student Response: The duck is the smallest.
    Teacher Comment: **How do you know the duck is small?**
        Student Response: The body of the duck seems smaller than the bodies of the other two birds.
    Teacher Comment: **Trace the word "small," then draw a line from the picture of the duck to the word "small."**

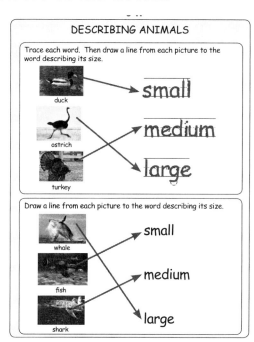

    Teacher Comment: **Which bird is the largest?**
        Student Response: The ostrich is the largest.
    Teacher Comment: **How do you know that the ostrich is the largest?**
        Student Response: The ostrich is the tallest bird. It can eat the leaves of large bushes and small trees. Its body is bigger than a turkey or a duck.
    Teacher Comment: **Trace the word "large," then draw a line from the picture of the ostrich to the word "large."**

    Teacher Comment: **Which bird is medium in size?**
        Student Response: The turkey is medium in size.
    Teacher Comment: **How do you know that the turkey is medium in size?**
        Student Response: The turkey is larger than the duck, but smaller than the ostrich.
    Teacher Comment: **Trace the word "medium," then draw a line from the picture of the turkey to the word "medium."**

Kindergarten Thinking Skills & Key Concepts — Teacher's Manual

Teacher Comment: **Name the three animals in the second group.**
Student Response: The animals are a whale, a fish, and a shark.
Teacher Comment: **Which animal is the largest?**
Student Response: The whale is the largest.
Teacher Comment: **How do you know that the whale is the largest?**
Student Response: The whale is largest animal in the sea.
Teacher Comment: **Draw a line from the whale to the word "large."**

Teacher Comment: **Which animal is the smallest?**
Student Response: The fish are the smallest.
Teacher Comment: **How do you know that the fish are the smallest?**
Student Response: The fish have smaller bodies than the shark and the whale.
Teacher Comment: **Draw a line from the fish to the word "small."**

Teacher Comment: **Which animal is medium in size compared to the others?**
Student Response: The shark is larger than the fish but smaller than the whale.
Teacher Comment: **Draw a line from the shark to the word "medium."**

Thinking about Thinking
Teacher Comment: **What do you think about to compare the size of animals?**
Student Response:
1. I look at the size of the animal compared to its surroundings.
2. I use what I know about the animal.
3. I find the largest and the smallest animals.
4. I decide which animal is smaller than the largest one and larger than the smallest.

Personal Application
Teacher Comment: **When is it important to compare the sizes of animals of the same kind?**
Student Response: I compare the sizes of animals to explain how they are different or to tell a story about them.

Page 95 – DESCRIBING ANIMALS

LESSON

Introduction
Teacher Comment: **We have learned to describe animals by their size.**

Stating the Objective
Teacher Comment: **In this lesson you will compare the size of four animals.**

Conducting the Lesson
Teacher Comment: **These photographs compare the size of four animals. Name these animals.**
Student Response: The animals are a giraffe, a camel, a shark, and a lizard.
Teacher Comment: **Which animal is the tallest?**
Student Response: The giraffe is the tallest.
Teacher Comment: **Write "giraffe" on the first blank line.**

Teacher Comment: **Which animal is the shortest?**
Student Response: The lizard is the shortest.
Teacher Comment: **Write "lizard" on the second blank line.**

Teacher Comment: **Which animal is larger than a lizard, but smaller than a camel?**

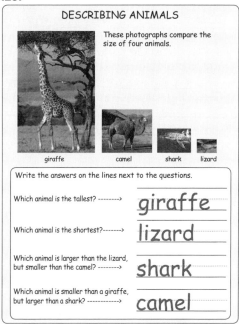

Student Response: The shark is larger than a lizard and smaller than a camel.
Teacher Comment: **Write the word "shark" on the third blank line.**

Teacher Comment: **Which animal is smaller than a giraffe, but larger than a shark?**
Student Response: The camel is smaller than a giraffe and larger than a shark.
Teacher Comment: **Write the word "camel" on the fourth blank line.**

Thinking about Thinking
Teacher Comment: **What do you think about to compare the size of animals?**
Student Response:
1. I look at the size of the animal compared to its surroundings.
2. I use what I know about the animal.
3. I find the largest and the smallest animals.
4. I decide which animal is smaller than the largest one and larger than the smallest.

Personal Application
Teacher Comment: **When is it important to compare the sizes of animals of the same kind?**
Student Response: I compare the sizes of animals to explain how they are different or to tell a story about them.

Page 96 – PARTS OF A DUCK

Introduction
Teacher Comment: **To describe animals we sometimes need to know the names of the parts of the animal and explain how each part is important for the animal to be healthy and to survive.**

LESSON

Stating the Objective
Teacher Comment: **In this lesson we will think about the parts of a duck, what each part does, and what would happen to the duck if that part was missing or damaged.**

Conducting the Lesson
Teacher Comment: **What part of the duck is needed for the duck to fly?**
Student Response: The duck needs wings to fly.
Teacher Comment: **Write the word "wings" on the top blank.**

Teacher Comment: **What would happen if the wings were missing or damaged?**
Student Response: The duck could not fly. It could not find food or escape from animals that could harm it.

Teacher Comment: **What parts of the duck are needed for the duck to find food?**
Student Response: The duck needs eyes to find food.
Teacher Comment: **Write the word "eyes" on the second blank.**

Teacher Comment: **What would happen if the eyes were missing or damaged?**
Student Response: The duck could not see to find food.

Teacher Comment: **What part of the duck is used to catch food?**
  Student Response: The duck needs a bill to catch food.
Teacher Comment: **Write the word "bill" on the third blank.**

Teacher Comment: **What would happen if the bill was missing or damaged?**
  Student Response: The duck could not catch food to eat.

Teacher Comment: **What part of the duck is under water to help the duck swim.**
  Student Response: The feet are under water.
Teacher Comment: **Its feet are flat and wide and are called webbed feet. Write the word "feet" on the bottom lines.**

Teacher Comment: **What would happen if the webbed feet were missing or damaged?**
  Student Response: The duck could not swim very fast to escape animals that might harm it. It would not be able to catch food as easily.

Thinking about Thinking
  Teacher Comment: **What did you think about to describe the parts of an animal?**
  Student Response:
  1. I looked at each part and named it correctly.
  2. I remembered what each part does.
  3. I thought about what each part did to help the animal be healthy and safe.

Personal Application
  Teacher Comment: **When is it important to describe the parts of an animal?**
  Student Response: I need to know the names of each part and what it does to describe the animal correctly or to tell a story about it.

Page 97 - SIMILAR ANIMALS

TEACHING SUGGESTIONS

- This lesson introduces the important characteristics "cold-blooded" and "warm-blooded." Use these terms to describe any animals that students study or read about. Continue to explain that warmth is necessary for survival whether the animal has warmth from its own body or must get it from its environment.

- Emphasize the words commonly used to describe similarities. Repeat words that show similarity (both, and, like, similar, resemble, also, etc.) and encourage students to use them in their responses.

- Students may not know the term "scale." Scales are tiny, hard pieces of skin that cover fish and reptiles.

- Some Teachers reinforce students' responses by writing their comments on the HOW ARE TWO THINGS ALIKE diagram shown in the appendix. See the example at the right. Use a transparency or draw the diagram on chart paper or display board. Students begin to associate their answers with the words that they see on the diagram. However, if writing on the diagram distracts young children from thinking about the topic, using this method may not be helpful.

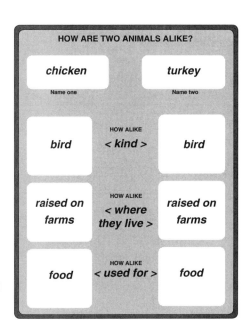

LESSON

Introduction

Teacher Comment: **In order to survive, animals need to have some warmth for their bodies to work. Some animals are warm-blooded. Their bodies make enough warmth to keep them alive. If you touch a warm-blooded animal, it feels warm, like a kitten.**
Some animals are cold-blooded. They do not make warmth in their bodies. They must get warmth from their surroundings. If you touch a cold-blooded animal, it feels cool, like a fish.
In this lesson you will add whether animals are warm-blooded or cold-blooded when you describe them.

Stating the Objective

Teacher Comment: **In this lesson you will look at a picture of an animal and then decide which of three animals is most like it.**

Conducting the Lesson

Teacher Comment: **Name the animals in the example.**
   Student Response: The four animals are a zebra, a camel, a giraffe, and a horse.

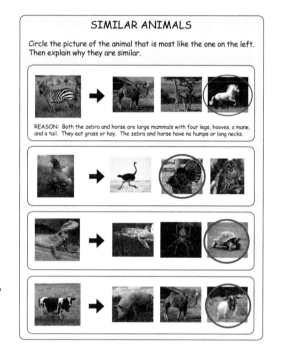

Teacher Comment: **The first animal is a zebra. A zebra is a warm-blooded animal**
Teacher Comment: **Tell your partner all the important things that you know about a zebra.**
   Student Response: A zebra is a large, warm-blooded animal. It has four legs with hooves, a mane, and a tail. It eats hay or grass. A zebra looks like a horse with stripes.
Teacher Comment: **Which of these animals is most like a zebra?**
   Student Response: The horse is most like a zebra.
Teacher Comment: **How is the horse most like a zebra?**
   Student Response: They are both warm-blooded animals. They have four legs with hooves, a mane, and a tail. They both eat hay or grass. They both run fast.
Teacher Comment: **How are the other two animals different from a zebra?**
   Student Response: A camel has humps and no stripes. A giraffe has a long neck and spots instead of stripes.
Teacher Comment: **Notice the circle around the horse to show that it is most like a zebra.**

Teacher Comment: **Look at the second row. Name the four animals.**
   Student Response: The animals are a chicken, an ostrich, a turkey, and an owl.
Teacher Comment: **The first picture shows a chicken. Tell your partner all the important things that you know about a chicken.**
   Student Response: A chicken is warm-blooded animal. It is a bird with feathers. It lays eggs. Chickens are raised by farmers to be sold as food. People eat the meat and eggs of a chicken.
Teacher Comment: **Which animal is most like a chicken?**
   Student Response: A turkey is most like a chicken.
Teacher Comment: **Why is a turkey most like a chicken?**
   Student Response: A turkey is also warm-blooded and lays eggs. They are both birds with long feathers and short legs. They are also raised by farmers to be sold as food.
Teacher Comment: **How are the other animals different from a chicken?**
   Student Response: An owl is a wild bird, but it is not used for food. An ostrich is a large bird that has longer legs and can move much faster than a chicken.
Teacher Comment: **Draw a circle around the turkey to show that it is most like a chicken.**

Teacher Comment: **Look at the third row. Name the four animals.**
  Student Response: The animals are a lizard, a shark, a spider, and a turtle.
Teacher Comment: **The first picture shows a lizard. Tell your partner all the important things that you know about a lizard.**
  Student Response: A lizard is a cold-blooded animal. It has four short legs and a long tail. Its body is long and scaly. Most lizards like to eat insects. They live in places where the temperature is usually warm most of the time. The skin of the lizard can be used to make leather, which can be used to make shoes, boots, or wallets.
Teacher Comment: **Which animal is most like a lizard?**
  Student Response: A turtle is most like a lizard.
Teacher Comment: **How is a turtle most like a lizard?**
  Student Response: A turtle also has a small body and four short legs. Both live where the temperature is usually warm most of the time. Both lay eggs.
Teacher Comment: **How are the other animals different from a lizard?**
  Student Response: A spider is a kind of bug with eight legs. A shark is a large fish that lives in water.
Teacher Comment: **Draw a circle around the turtle.**

- Continue this dialog for the group with the cow, pig, camel, and goat.

Thinking About Thinking
  Teacher Comment: **What did you think about to decide which animal is most like another one?**
  Student Response:
  1. I recalled the important details of the first animal (its appearance, where it lives, what kind of animal it is, warm or cold-blooded, how it moves, etc.).
  2. I looked for similar details in the other animals.
  3. I selected the animal that has most of the same details.
  4. I checked to see that other animals do not fit the important details.

Personal Application
  Teacher Comment: **When is it important to understand how animals are alike?**
  Student Response: I need to understand the needs of animals that we find at the zoo or the pet store, to care for pets properly. I need to understand how similar animals living in the same environment get the food, water, air, and safety that they need to survive.

Page 98 - SIMILAR ANIMALS

TEACHING SUGGESTIONS
- Emphasize the wording commonly used to describe similarities. Repeat words that show similarity (both, and, like, similar, resemble, also, etc.) and encourage students to use them in their responses.

- Students may need more explanation of the structure and function of a backbone. Use pictures of skeletons of various animals and ask students to locate their own backbones. The terms "vertebra" and "spine" may be used.

- Some Teachers reinforce students' responses by writing their comments on the HOW ARE TWO THINGS ALIKE diagram shown in the appendix. See the example at the right. Use a transparency or draw the diagram on chart paper or display board. Students begin to associate their answers with the words that they see on the diagram. However, if writing on the diagram distracts young children from thinking about the topic, using this method may not be helpful.

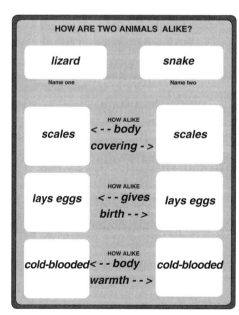

LESSON

Introduction

- Display a skeleton of an animal.
  Teacher Comment: **We have practiced selecting animals that are similar. It is important to know whether or not an animal has a backbone. A backbone is the stack of small bones that connect the brain to the other parts of an animal's body. The backbone strengthens its body and carries the nerves that allow the animal to move. Most large animals have a backbone. Animals that don't have a backbone have different body parts to strengthen the animal.**

Stating the Objective

Teacher Comment: **In this lesson you will explain how two animals are alike.**

Conducting the Lesson

Teacher Comment: **Explain how a lizard and a snake are alike.**
Student Response: Both are cold-blooded, have backbones, and have scaly bodies. Their babies are hatched from eggs. Both lizards and snakes eat insects.
Teacher Comment: **What did you describe to explain how these animals are alike?**
Student Response: I described its skin, that it is cold-blooded, that it has a backbone, and that it hatches from eggs.
Teacher Comment: **Trace and copy the words "lizard" and "snake."**

Teacher Comment: **The next exercise shows an ostrich and a turkey. Explain how they are alike.**
Student Response: Both are large, feathered, warm-blooded animals with backbones. Their babies are hatched from eggs. Both eat grain.

Teacher Comment: **Trace and copy the words "ostrich" and "turkey."**

Teacher Comment: **Look at the next pair of animals. Explain how these animals are alike.**
Student Response: Both are large mammals. They are warm-blooded animals with backbones and four hoofed feet. The females give live birth. They are strong, can carry heavy loads, people ride them, and they can walk long distances.
Teacher Comment: **Trace and copy the words "camel" and "horse."**

- Continue this dialog for "shark" and "goldfish."

Thinking About Thinking

Teacher Comment: **What did you explain about animals to tell how they are alike?**
Student Response:
1. I explained its appearance, whether it is warm- or cold-blooded, whether it hatches or gives live birth, where it lives, how it moves, and its body covering.
2. I matched details that both animals have.
3. I checked to see that I have included all the important details of both animals.

Personal Application

Teacher Comment: **When is it important to understand how animals are alike?**
Student Response: I need to understand how animals are alike to understand the needs of animals that we find at the zoo or the pet store. I need to understand how to care for pets properly. I need to understand how animals living in the same environment get food, water, air, and the safety they need to survive.

Page 99 - SIMILARITIES AND DIFFERENCES

TEACHING SUGGESTIONS

- Emphasize the difference between "comparing" (describing how two things are alike) and "contrasting" (explaining how two things are different). Correct mistaken usage of the terms and acknowledge students' correct use of these terms.

- Emphasize the wording commonly used to describe similarities and differences. Repeat words that show similarity (both, and, like, similar, resemble, also, etc.) and encourage students to use them in their responses. Explain the term "unlike" and encourage students use words that cue differences (but, not, different, opposite, and unlike).

- To help young children express contrast, emphasize the use of the conjunction "but."

  Example: Chickens have beaks, but ducks have bills. Explain that "but" is a signal word to alert the reader or listener that what comes after it will be different than what came before it. Encourage students to use this sentence pattern and acknowledge students' unprompted statements expressing contrast using this syntax.

- Review the terms "cold-blooded" and "warm-blooded." Explain the effect of this difference on the survival needs of animals.

- For young children the terms "backbone" or "vertebra" may be new concepts. Discuss with students the significance and function of a backbone.

- Optional story telling after the lesson: Select a common story or fairy tale about animals, such as *Are You My Mother?* by P.D. Eastman. Ask students to retell the story about another animal, such as a duck and a duckling, instead of a mother bird and a baby bird. What interesting animals might the duckling meet? How is the revised story different from the original? (Since the duckling's home is in the water, he will ask different animals or things whether they are his mother. He must get home another way.)

- When contrasting animals, students sometimes answer with a detail about only one of the animals. For example, if the student answers that the chicken lives on a farm, confirm that it is correct that the chicken is a farm animal. Then ask whether a duck is a farm animal. The student then realizes that a duck flies freely from one pond to another and is not usually kept on a farm. It is usually a wild animal. The student has now contrasted where the animals live.

LESSON

Introduction
Teacher Comment: **In the last lesson we explained how two animals are alike.**

Stating the Objective
Teacher Comment: **In this lesson you will explain how two animals are alike and how they are different.**

Conducting the Lesson
Teacher Comment: **You see a chicken and a duck. How are these animals alike?**
  Student Response: Both are birds, babies hatch from eggs. Both are warm-blooded and have backbones. They can be pets or raised on farms for food. Both are about the same size and can come in many different colors. Both eat small plants and insects.
Teacher Comment: **How are these animals different?**
  Student Response: Ducks live near the water, but chickens do not. Chickens have beaks, but ducks have bills. Ducks can fly great distances, but chickens cannot. Ducks are good swimmers, but chickens do not swim.
Teacher Comment: **Trace and copy the words "chicken" and "ducks."**

Teacher Comment: **In the second exercise you see a spider and a lizard. How are these animals alike?**
  Student Response: They are both cold-blooded and lay eggs. Both run quickly and hide.
Teacher Comment: **How are these animals different?**
  Student Response: A lizard has four legs and a tail, but a spider has eight legs and no tail. A spider catches its food in a web, but a lizard catches its food with its tongue.
Teacher Comment: **Trace and copy the words "lizard" and "spider."**

Thinking About Thinking
Teacher Comment: **What did you explain about animals to tell how they are alike or different?**
Student Response:
1. I explained their appearance, whether they are warm- or cold-blooded, whether they hatch or give live birth, where they live, how they move, and their body covering.
2. I identified similar details of the two animals.
3. I identified the different details in the two animals.
4. I checked to see that I have identified the important details of both animals.

Personal Application
Teacher Comment: **When is it important to explain how animals are alike?**
Student Response: I need to understand the needs of animals that we find at the zoo or the pet store. I need to care for pets properly.
Teacher Comment: **When is it important to explain how animals are different?**
Student Response: I must tell how animals are different to keep myself or someone else from getting them confused.

Page 100-101 - KINDS OF ANIMALS

TEACHING SUGGESTIONS
- One page is commonly sufficient for one 20-30 minute session in order to have time for the "Thinking About Thinking" and "Personal Application" discussions. If more than one page is done in one session, conduct the "Thinking About Thinking" and "Personal Application" discussions at the end of the session, <u>not</u> at the end of each exercise.
- Remind students of the characteristics of birds, fish, mammals, and reptiles. The glossary at the end of the student book has a definition of terms. Have the students prepare a bulletin board display with pictures of animals that belong to the various classes.

LESSON

Introduction
Teacher Comment: **There are many kinds of animals. In this lesson we will study four kinds of animals: birds, mammals, fish, and reptiles. All these animals have a backbone, but other characteristics make them different.**

- Show some pictures of birds.

    Teacher Comment: **Birds lay eggs which must be kept warm until the baby birds hatch. Birds have feathers to keep their bodies warm. An ostrich and a turkey are birds.**

- Show some pictures of mammals.

    Teacher Comment: **Mammal mothers carry their babies inside their bodies and make milk for them. Most mammals have hair on their bodies. Horses, cows, dogs, and cats are mammals. Both mammals and the birds are warm-blooded animals. Because they have some heat in their bodies, they can live in places that are not too cold or too hot and do not have to depend on their surroundings for warmth.**

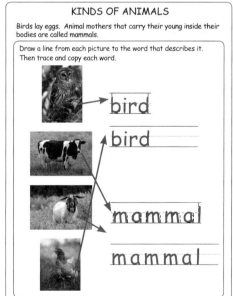

Stating the Objective
Teacher Comment: **In this lesson you will look at a picture of an animal and decide what kind of animal it is.**

Conducting the Lesson
   Teacher Comment: **Name the animal in the top picture.**
      Student Response: The top picture shows an owl.
   Teacher Comment: **What kind of animal is an owl?**
      Student Response: An owl is a bird.
   Teacher Comment: **Draw a line from the picture of the owl to the word "bird." Trace and copy the word "bird."**

   Teacher Comment: **Name the animal in the second picture.**
      Student Response: The second picture shows a cow.
   Teacher Comment: **What kind of animal is a cow?**
      Student Response: A cow is a mammal.
   Teacher Comment: **Draw a line from the picture of the cow to the word "mammal." Trace and copy the word "mammal."**

- Continue this dialog to discuss goat and chicken.

   Teacher Comment: **Turn to page 101.**

Introduction
   Teacher Comment: **Cold-blooded animals must get warmth from their surroundings. Since fish are in water all the time, the temperature of the water usually gives fish enough warmth to survive. A reptile is also a cold-blooded animal. Most reptiles live on land. In cold weather they must find shelter to have enough warmth. Both fish and reptiles lay eggs.**

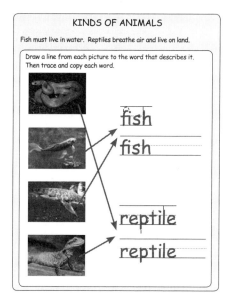

   Teacher Comment: **Name the animal in the top picture**
      Student Response: The top picture shows a snake.
   Teacher Comment: **What kind of animal is a snake?**
      Student Response: A snake is a reptile.
   Teacher Comment: **What details let you know that the snake is a reptile?**
      Student Response: The snake lives on land.
   Teacher Comment: **Draw a line from the picture of the snake to the word "reptile." Trace and copy the word "reptile."**

   Teacher Comment: **Name the animal in the second picture**
      Student Response: The second picture shows a goldfish.
   Teacher Comment: **What kind of animal is a goldfish?**
      Student Response: A goldfish is a fish.
   Teacher Comment: **What details let you know that the animal is a fish?**
      Student Response: The fish lives in water.
   Teacher Comment: **Draw a line from the picture of the goldfish to the word "fish." Trace and copy the word "fish."**

- Continue this dialog to discuss shark and lizard.

Thinking About Thinking
   Teacher Comment: **What did you think about to decide what kind of animal is shown in the picture?**
      Student Response:
      1. I looked at each picture and identified the animal.
      2. I remembered the important details about that animal (appearance, whether it is warm- or cold- blooded, where it lives, how it moves, whether it hatches or gives live birth to babies, and whether it has a backbone).
      3. I looked for the word that describes that kind of animal.

Personal Application
   Teacher Comment: **When is it important to explain what kinds of animals are alike?**
      Student Response: I need to explain the needs of different kinds of animals to tell about pets or zoo animals; to know what to pay attention to in books, movies, or television shows about animals; to recognize examples of common animals as being fish, birds, reptiles, or mammals.

Kindergarten Thinking Skills & Key Concepts   Teacher's Manual

Page 102 - KINDS OF ANIMALS

TEACHING SUGGESTIONS

- Use the terms "groups," "types," "kind of," and "classes" to help students conceptualize classification. Encourage students to use these words in their discussions.

- Remind students of the characteristics of birds, fish, mammals, and reptiles. The glossary at the end of the student book has a definition of terms.

- To extend this lesson, prepare a bulletin board display with pictures of animals that belong to the various classes. Use the branching diagram (#11) in the appendix as a guide.

LESSON

Introduction
    Teacher Comment: **In our last lessons we learned about four kinds of animals: birds, fish, mammals, and reptiles.**

Stating the Objective
    Teacher Comment: **In this lesson you will match animal pictures to the word that tells what kind of animal it is**.

Conducting the lesson
    Teacher Comment: **What are the animals in the first picture?**
      Student Response: Those animals are fish.
    Teacher Comment: **Notice that an arrow is drawn from the picture of the fish to the word "fish." Trace and copy the word "fish."**

    Teacher Comment: **Name the second animal.**
      Student Response: That animal is a pig.
    Teacher Comment: **What kind of animal is a pig?**
      Student Response: A pig is a mammal.
    Teacher Comment: **Draw an arrow from the pig to the word "mammal." Trace and copy the word "mammal."**

    Teacher Comment: **Name the animal in the third picture.**
      Student Response: That animal is a turtle.
    Teacher Comment: **What kind of animal is a turtle?**
      Student Response: A turtle is a reptile with a thick shell.
    Teacher Comment: **Draw a line from the turtle to the word "reptile." Trace and copy the word "reptile."**

    Teacher Comment: **Name the last animal.**
      Student Response: That animal is an owl.
    Teacher Comment: **What kind of animal is an owl.**
      Student Response: An owl is a bird.
    Teacher Comment: **Draw a line from the owl to the word "bird." Trace and copy the word "bird."**

Thinking about Thinking
    Teacher Comment: **What did you think about to decide what kind of animal is shown in the picture?**
      Student Response:
      1. I looked at each picture and identified the animal.
      2. I remembered the important details about that animal (appearance, whether it is warm- or cold-blooded, where it lives, how it moves, whether it hatches or gives live birth to babies, and whether it has a backbone).
      3. I looked for the word that describes that kind of animal.

Personal Application
    Teacher Comment: **When is it important to know what kind of animal you describe?**
      Student Response: I name the kind of animal to describe it correctly and to read or write about it.

Kindergarten Thinking Skills & Key Concepts Teacher's Manual

Page 103 - KINDS OF ANIMALS

TEACHING SUGGESTIONS

- "Mammals" and "reptiles" are abstract concepts for most young children. Since they have heard these terms several times in previous exercises, students should begin to use them independently. Use the terms "mammals" and "reptiles" often in these activities and in other contexts and encourage students to do so. Acknowledge students' unprompted use of these terms.

- As students explain which animal is not like the others, they are contrasting the exception. Encourage students to use words that show how the animal is different: but, not, different, instead of, and unlike.

LESSON

Introduction
Teacher Comment: **We have named various kinds of animals.**

Stating the Objective
Teacher Comment: **In this lesson you will identify an animal that is not the same kind as the others.**

Conducting the Lesson

Teacher Comment: **Name the animals in first row.**
  Student Response: A chicken, a duck, a pig and a turkey.
Teacher Comment: **Discuss with your partner how three of the animals are alike.**

Teacher Comment: **How are three of the animals alike?**
  Student Response: A chicken, a turkey, and a duck lay eggs. They have feathers. They all have wings and can fly through the air.
Teacher Comment: **What word describes this kind of animal?**
  Student Response: A chicken, a duck, and a turkey are birds.
Teacher Comment: **Trace the word "birds."**

Teacher Comment: **Which animal doesn't fit that group?**
  Student Response: A pig is not a bird.
Teacher Comment: **Why is the pig an exception to the group "bird?"**
  Student Response: A pig is a mammal. It gives birth to live babies. It has hair, not feathers. It has legs, not wings. It lives on land and cannot fly.
Teacher Comment: **Mark an "X" through the picture of the pig.**

Teacher Comment: **Name the animals in the second row.**
  Student Response: The animals are a cow, a horse, an owl, and a zebra.
Teacher Comment: **Discuss with your partner how three of the animals are alike.**

Teacher Comment: **How are three of the animals alike?**
  Student Response: A cow, a horse, and a zebra all are four legged animals that walk on hooves. They give live birth and make milk for their babies. They all have hair. They all live on the ground.
Teacher Comment: **What word describes this kind of animal?**
  Student Response: A cow, horse, and a zebra are mammals.
Teacher Comment: **Trace the word "mammals."**
Teacher Comment: **Which animal doesn't fit that group?**
  Student Response: An owl is not a mammal.
Teacher Comment: **Why is the owl an exception to the group "mammals?"**
  Student Response: An owl is a bird. It lays eggs and has feathers instead of hair. It lives in trees, not on the ground. It flies instead of running.
Teacher Comment: **Mark an "X" through the picture of the owl.**

Teacher Comment: **Name the animals in the third row.**
   Student Response: The animals are a shark, a lizard, a snake, and a turtle.
Teacher Comment: **Discuss with your partner how three of the animals are alike.**

Teacher Comment: **How are three of the animals alike?**
   Student Response: A lizard, snake, and turtle lay eggs. They are cold-blooded animals that move by crawling.
Teacher Comment: **What word describes this kind of animal?**
Student Response: A lizard, snake, and turtle are reptiles.
Teacher Comment: **Trace the word "reptiles."**

Teacher Comment: **Which animal doesn't fit that group?**
   Student Response: A shark is not a reptile.
Teacher Comment: **Why is the shark an exception to the group "reptiles?"**
   Student Response: A shark is a large fish, not a reptile. It lives in the ocean not on land. It swims with fins instead of crawling.
Teacher Comment: **Mark an "X" through the picture of the shark.**

Thinking about Thinking
Teacher Comment: **What did you say to explain that these animals are the same kind?**
Student Response:
1. I looked at pictures of various animals and identified the important details (its appearance and skin covering, whether it is warm- or cold-blooded, whether it has a back bone, whether it hatches or gives live birth, where it lives, and how it moves).
2. I looked for the word that describes the kind of animal that has those important details.
3. I identified the animal that does not fit that group and explained why.

Personal Application
Teacher Comment: **When is it important to explain how an animal is different from another group?**
Student Response: I explain how an animal is different to show why the needs of different kinds of pets or zoo animals may be different, to know what to pay attention to in books, movies, or televisions shows about animals.

Page 104 - KINDS OF ANIMALS

LESSON

Introduction
   Teacher Comment: **In the last lesson we found animals that were not the same kind as the rest of the group.**

Stating the Objective
   Teacher Comment: **In this lesson you will complete a sentence that describes a kind of animal.**

Conducting the Lesson
   Teacher Comment: **Name the animal in the top box.**
      Student Response: That animal is a duck.
   Teacher Comment: **Trace the sentence, "A duck is a bird."**

   Teacher Comment: **Name the animal in the second box.**
      Student Response: That animal is a snake.
   Teacher Comment: **Use words from the WORD BOX to write a sentence that tells what kind of animal it is.**

   Teacher Comment: **Name the animal in the third box.**
      Student Response: That animal is a zebra.
   Teacher Comment: **Use words from the WORD BOX to write a sentence that tells what kind of animal it is.**

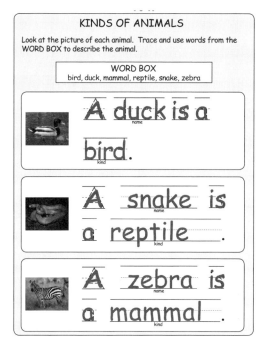

Thinking about Thinking
   Teacher Comment: **What did you think about to describe the kind of animal shown in the picture?**
      Student Response:
      1. I looked at each picture and identified the animal.
      2. I remembered the important details about that animal (appearance, whether it is warm- or cold-blooded, where it lives, how it moves, whether it hatches or gives live birth to babies, and whether it has a backbone).
      3. I looked for the word that describes that kind of animal.
      4. I finished a sentence that names the animal and tells what kind of animal it is.

Personal Application
   Teacher Comment: **When is it important to describe a kind of animal?**
      Student Response: I name the kind of animal to describe it correctly and write about it.

CHAPTER NINE – THINKING ABOUT JOBS (Pages 106-114)

TEACHING ABOUT JOBS

CURRICULUM APPLICATIONS
Health: Identify people who produce and distribute food; identify health and emergency workers
Social Studies: Define a consumer as a user of goods and services; identify how a family depends upon products and services to meet its needs; identify some job roles in the community; cite examples of community needs and services; recognize the differences between producing and selling goods

LANGUAGE INTEGRATION ACTIVITIES

- A list of jobs described in this chapter is provided in the appendix. To help students associate the word with the picture of the job, enlarge this list for display and refer to the term for various jobs as you teach the lesson.

- Drawing: Each student may draw a person's job. Label the drawing with a description of that job. Students' drawings may be used to create a "big book."

- Listening: Prior to a lesson that features a job, read aloud a non-fiction picture book about that job. Language experiences with picture books extend this lesson and demonstrate how various occupations provide goods and services to meet people's needs. After discussing any of the picture books ask the following questions:
  Are there any new ideas about (any job) that we learned from this story?
  What ideas or details about (any job) did you learn from the pictures?

- Select a common story or fairy tale about a job, such as *The Shoemaker and the Elves* by Jacob Grimm. Ask students to retell the story about another job (e.g. a construction worker instead of a shoemaker). Discuss how the revised story is different from the original. For example, how might the elves help a construction worker and what might a construction worker make for the elves in return?

- Drama: Collect or construct hats/articles used in different professions. Ask students to role play as the worker and the customer seeking goods or services.

- Encourage students to describe examples of farmers, teachers, or police officers from their local community. Identify individual farmers, teachers, or police officers from various ethnic backgrounds.

TEACHING SUGGESTIONS
- Students may not commonly use the term "occupation." Discuss with students common synonyms (jobs, livelihood, career, work, etc.).

- Emphasize the terms that are commonly used with each job and encourage students to use those terms.

- Teachers may use the graphic organizers shown on page 93 for bulletin board displays, student art work, or end-of-unit summary lessons.

MENTAL MODEL
A mental model is a framework for understanding a concept. It outlines the characteristics that one must identify to describe or define a concept. After completing this chapter, each kindergarten student will have applied this mental model to the jobs in the lessons. A mental model helps a student:

- Anticipate what he or she needs to know to understand a new job
- Remember the characteristics of a job
- State a clear definition or write an adequate description of a job
- Explain a job to someone else

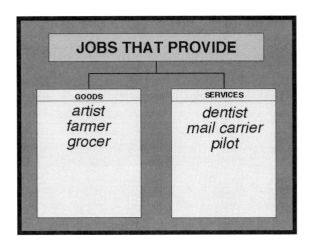
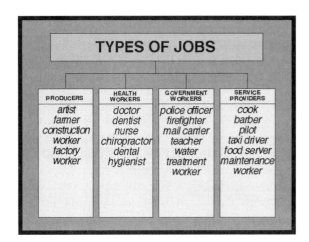
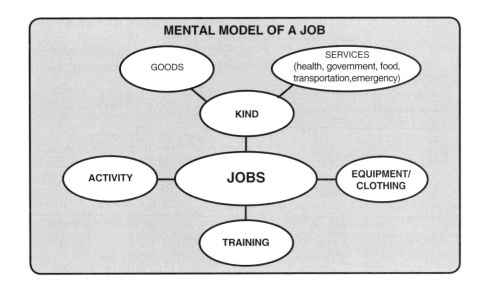

Kindergarten Thinking Skills & Key Concepts — Teacher's Manual

Page 106 - DESCRIBING JOBS

LESSON

Introduction
  Teacher Comment: **People in our community have jobs that help our families get what they need. Some people make things that the rest of us need. Some people are paid to do something for us. They provide a service. Some people work for the government to provide a service that the whole community needs.**

Stating the Objective
  Teacher Comment: **I will describe a job and you will select it.**

Conducting the Lesson
  Teacher Comment: **I will describe one of the jobs. You will select the picture that fits the description. This person grows fruits or vegetables or raises animals for us to eat. He or she cares for large fields with lots of trees or plants. He or she must be sure that his or her plants or animals have enough water and food to grow healthy and large. He or she takes care of his or her crops or his or her animals to be sure that weeds, insects, or disease do not keep them from growing. He or she uses large machines, such as tractors, plows, and sprayers to grow large amounts of food. He or she has learned about plants and animals from other farmers, by growing up on a farm, or by going to school for a long time. He or she must keep good records about how his or her crops or animals grow and how to sell them for a good price.**

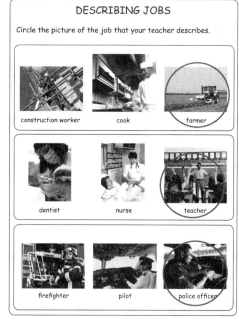

- Ask students to decide with their partners which job has been described.

  Teacher Comment: **What do we call this job?**
    Student Response: This person is a farmer.
  Teacher Comment: **Circle the picture of the farmer.**

  Teacher Comment: **What clues let you know that the person in this picture is a farmer?**
    Student Response: His tractor and field show that he is a farmer.
  Teacher Comment: **Why don't the other jobs fit this description?**
    Student Response: The construction worker doesn't work with food at all. The cook prepares food, but doesn't grow it.

  Teacher Comment: **Look at the second group of photos on this page. Select the picture that fits this description. This person helps boys and girls learn things they need to know: how to read, write, draw, play music, and get along with other people. He or she helps students learn to use numbers and shapes and to understand our city, our country, and nature. He or she works with the children from early morning to the middle of the afternoon. When the children leave, he or she checks their work and plans what they will do on the next day. He or she understands how children learn and how to explain things to them easily. He or she uses books, maps, computers, pictures, and a chalkboard to help children understand ideas. He or she went to school for a long time to learn how to do this well.**

- Ask students to decide with their partners which job has been described.

  Teacher Comment: **What do we call this job?**
    Student Response: This person is a teacher.
  Teacher Comment: **Circle the picture of the teacher.**

  Teacher Comment: **What clues let you know that the person in this picture is a teacher?**
    Student Response: The chalkboard behind him and the children in front of him show that he is working in a

school. The childrens' raised hands shows that they are answering questions that he has asked.
Teacher Comment: **Why don't the other jobs fit this description?**
Student Response: The dentist and the nurse work with one person at a time. Their surroundings show the tools for taking care of teeth or a sick person. Both the dentist and the nurse wear clothing to help them stay very clean. The teacher wears ordinary clothes.

Teacher Comment: **Select the picture that fits the description. This law enforcement officer protects people and property and helps prevent crime. He or she sometimes rides in a car or on a motorcycle, wears a uniform, and has a badge to let people know that he or she is an official. He or she studies laws and learns how to keep himself or herself and other people safe.**

- Ask students to decide with their partners which job has been described.

    Teacher Comment: **What do we call this job?**
    Student Response: This person is a police officer.
    Teacher Comment: **Circle the picture of the police officer.**

    Teacher Comment: **What clues let you know that the person in this picture is a police officer?**
    Student Response: His uniform shows that he is a police officer.
    Teacher Comment: **Why don't the other jobs fit this description?**
    Student Response: The heavy clothing and helmet protect the firefighter. The surroundings of the firefighters show that they use equipment to put out fires. The pilot sits in front of the equipment of an airplane.

Thinking About Thinking
Teacher Comment: **What did you look for when you picked out the job that was described?**
Student Response:
1. I remembered the important details of the job. (activities, goods or services, training, equipment, surroundings, etc.).
2. I found the important details in the pictures.
3. I checked that the photographs of other jobs do not show those important details.

Personal Application
Teacher Comment: **When is it important to understand what people do in their jobs?**
Student Response: I describe jobs to explain what friends or family members do for a living, to describe commercials, to describe businesses to a newcomer.

Page 107 - DESCRIBING JOBS

- Students may not commonly use the term "occupation." Discuss with students common synonyms (jobs, livelihood, career, work, etc.).

LESSON

Introduction
Teacher Comment: **We have selected a job from its description.**

Staring the Objective
Teacher Comment: **In this lesson you will look at a photograph and describe the job that the person does.**

Conducting the Lesson
Teacher Comment: **Look at the first picture. Name this job and describe it to your partner.**
Student Response: This picture shows a doctor. A doctor helps people feel better and can decide what medicine or treatment a person needs in order to heal. He or she works in offices or hospitals and sometimes wears special clothing. A doctor must go to school for a long time to learn how people's bodies work. He or she uses a thermometer to take people's temperature and uses other equipment such as scales, microscopes, stethoscopes, cotton, and needles.
Teacher Comment: **Trace and copy the word "doctor."**

Teacher Comment: **What details do you describe to explain that the person in the picture is a doctor?**
Student Response: His clothing shows that he keeps his surroundings very clean. His stethoscope helps him hear the baby's heart so that he can tell whether the child is healthy.

Teacher Comment: **Look at the second photograph on this page. Name this job and describe it to your partner.**
Student Response: This picture shows a pilot. A pilot controls the speed and direction of an airplane. He or she is the driver of the plane. He or she and other specially trained airplane workers sit in the cockpit (the front section) and look out of a windshield like the one in cars. He or she has to learn how a plane operates and how to read the dials and lights that show that the plane is safe and operating correctly. He or she must know the correct direction to steer the plane where it must go. A pilot wears a special uniform.
Teacher Comment: **Trace and copy the word "pilot."**

Teacher Comment: **What details do you describe to explain that the person in the picture is a pilot?**
Student Response: The pilot sits in front of the controls of an airplane. The windows in front of them allow them to see where the plane is going. Pilots wear uniforms that let the traveler know who flies the plane.

Teacher Comment: **Look at the bottom photograph. Name this job and describe it to your partner.**
Student Response: This picture shows a mail carrier. A mail carrier wears a uniform and delivers letters, bills, advertisements, magazines, and packages to homes and places of business.
Teacher Comment: **Trace and copy the word "mail carrier."**

Teacher Comment: **What details do you describe to explain that the person in the picture is a mail carrier?**
Student Response: His truck carries the mail that he is delivering. In his hand he holds a letter which he will deliver. His uniform is like other mail carriers.

Thinking About Thinking
Teacher Comment: **What did you describe to explain this job?**
Student Response:
1. I recalled the important details of the job (what the worker does, training, equipment, and special clothes).
2. I checked that I described all those important details.
3. I checked that I have given enough details to keep the job that I am describing from being confused with another job.

Personal Application
Teacher Comment: **When is it important to describe people or jobs well?**
Student Response: I describe jobs to explain what friends or family members do for a living, to describe businesses to a newcomer.

Kindergarten Thinking Skills & Key Concepts   Teacher's Manual

Pages 108-109 - DESCRIBING JOBS

TEACHING SUGGESTIONS
- One page is commonly sufficient for one 20-30 minute session in order to have time for the "Thinking About Thinking" and "Personal Application" discussions. If more than one page is done in one session, conduct the "Thinking About Thinking" and "Personal Application" discussions at the end of the session, not at the end of each exercise.

LESSON

Introduction
　Teacher Comment: **In the last lesson we described jobs.**

Stating the Objective
　Teacher Comment: **In this lesson you are going to match the pictures of the jobs to the words for them.**

Conducting the Lesson
　Teacher Comment: **Name the first job.**
　　Student Response: The first picture shows a barber.
　Teacher Comment: **What details show that the person is a barber?**
　　Student Response: He has a hair clipper in his hand. He is cutting a boy's hair.
　Teacher Comment: **Notice that an arrow is drawn from the picture of the barber to the word "barber." Trace and copy the word "barber."**

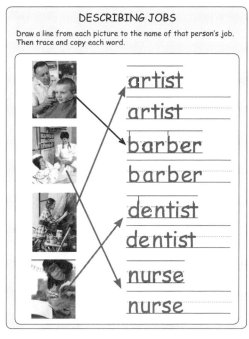

　Teacher Comment: **Name the job shown in the second picture.**
　　Student Response: The second picture shows a nurse.
　Teacher Comment: **What details show that the person is a nurse?**
　　Student Response: The bed and the equipment behind her show that she works in a hospital. She is checking the health of a patient who is in bed.
　Teacher Comment: **Draw a line from the picture to the word "nurse." Trace and copy the word "nurse."**

　Teacher Comment: **Name the job shown in the third picture.**
　　Student Response: The third picture shows an artist.
　Teacher Comment: **What details show that the person is an artist?**
　　Student Response: The person is painting a picture.
　Teacher Comment: **Draw a line from the picture to the word "artist." Trace and copy the word "artist."**

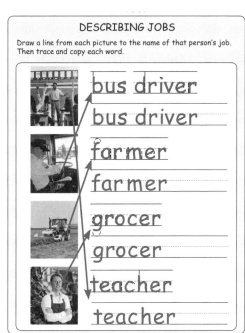

- Continue this dialog for dentist and for the jobs on page 109.

Thinking About Thinking
　Teacher Comment: **How did you decide which word belonged with each picture?**
　　Student Response:
　　1. I saw what the person was doing.
　　2. I looked at the clothes, the equipment, and the surroundings.
　　3. I named the job.
　　4. I found the word for the job.

Personal Application
　Teacher Comment: **When is it important to find the word for a job?**
　　Student Response: I find words for jobs in order to write about them.

© 2015 The Critical Thinking Co.™ • www.CriticalThinking.com • 800-458-4849

Page 110 - SIMILAR JOBS

TEACHING SUGGESTIONS
- Emphasize the wording commonly used to describe similarities. Repeat words that show similarity (both, and, like, similar, resemble, also, etc.) and encourage students to use them in their responses. Explain the term "unlike" and encourage students to use words that cue differences (but, not, different, opposite, and unlike).
- Some Teachers reinforce students' responses by writing their comments on the HOW ARE TWO THINGS ALIKE diagram shown in the appendix. See the example at the right. Use a transparency or draw the diagram on chart paper or display board. Students begin to associate their answers with the words that they see on the diagram. However, if writing on the diagram distracts young children from thinking about the topic, using this method may not be helpful.

LESSON

Introduction
Teacher Comment: **We have described many jobs.**

Stating the Objective
Teacher Comment: **In this lesson, you will find a job that is most like another one.**

Conducting the Lesson
Teacher Comment: **Name the jobs in the example.**
   Student Response: The jobs are dentist, doctor, mail carrier, and teacher.
Teacher Comment: **The first picture is dentist. Tell your partner all the important things you know about a dentist.**
   Student Response: Dentists clean and fix teeth. They go to school for a long time to learn how to keep teeth healthy. They use special tools or medicines to treat tooth and gum disease or injuries to our teeth. They wear special clothes, work in offices, and can be male or female.
Teacher Comment: **Which job on the right is most like a dentist?**
   Student Response: The doctor is most like a dentist because doctors help us keep our bodies healthy. They go to school for a long time to learn how all the parts of our bodies work, what healthy bodies need, and how to treat injuries or illnesses. They use special tools or medicines.
Teacher Comment: **What clues let you know that a doctor is most like a dentist?**
   Student Response: Both provide a health service to our community, must have special training, tools or supplies, wear special clothes, can be male or female, and work in offices or hospitals.
Teacher Comment: **How are the other jobs different from the dentist's?**
   Student Response: The teacher teaches students. He or she works in a classroom, not an office, and does not work on teeth. The mail carrier delivers mail and does not treat illness or injury. He or she walks outside or drives a special truck, but does not work in an office.

Teacher Comment: **Name the jobs in the second row.**
   Student Response: The jobs are bus driver, grocer, nurse, and pilot.
Teacher Comment: **The first picture is a bus driver. Tell your partner all the important things you know about a bus driver.**
   Student Response: A bus driver drives a large vehicle to take passengers on the same roads each day. He or she usually wears a uniform. People pay to ride the bus.

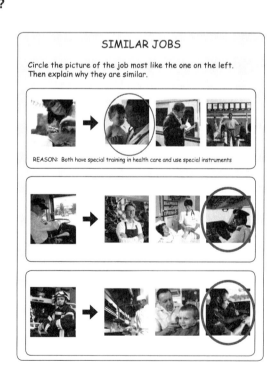

Teacher Comment: **Which job on the right is most like a bus driver?**
Student Response: A pilot is most like a bus driver.
Teacher Comment: **Circle the picture of the pilot.**

Teacher Comment: **What clues let you know that a pilot is most like a bus driver?**
Student Response: Both drive a vehicle that people pay to ride. Both wear a uniform. They take passengers a long distance at the same time each day.
Teacher Comment: **How are the other jobs different from the bus driver's?**
Student Response: The nurse helps sick people, the grocer sells food. Neither drives a vehicle that carries paying passengers.

Teacher Comment: **Name the jobs shown in the last row.**
Student Response: The jobs are firefighter, cook, barber, and police officer.
Teacher Comment: **The first picture is a firefighter. Tell your partner all the important things you know about a firefighter.**
Student Response: A firefighter is trained to put out fires, to rescue people from burning buildings, and to prevent fires from happening. Firefighters wear heavy clothing made to protect them from the heat and flames of a fire. They wear helmets and goggles to protect their heads and eyes. They wear small masks over their noses and mouths to keep from breathing smoke. They use hatchets to open doors to get people out or to get into rooms that are on fire. They use ladders to get to high places. They use hoses to bring enough water to put out the fire.
Teacher Comment: **Which job on the right is most like a firefighter.**
Student Response: A police officer is most like a firefighter.
Teacher Comment: **Circle the picture of the police officer.**

Teacher Comment: **What clues let you know that a police officer is most like a firefighter?**
Student Response: Both are government jobs. Both help keep us, our homes and belongings safe from harm. Both wear uniforms and use special tools and vehicles in their jobs. Both jobs may be dangerous. Both find out (investigate) information to prevent harm. They use cars or trucks with sirens and alarm lights to help people quickly.
Teacher Comment: **How are the other jobs different from the firefighter's.**
Student Response: The barber and cook do not have dangerous jobs. They do not help keep us, our homes and belongings safe from harm. They work in businesses, not for the government.

Thinking About Thinking
Teacher Comment: **What did you think about to compare different jobs?**
Student Response:
1. I recalled the important details of each of the jobs (their appearance, special equipment, and what they do).
2. I matched details that both jobs have.
3. I checked to see that the others are not as alike.

Personal Application
Teacher Comment: **When is it important to tell how jobs are alike?**
Student Response: I tell how jobs are alike to tell about jobs that are similar to ones I already understand; or to explain a job to someone who is unfamiliar with it.

Page 111 - SIMILAR JOBS

TEACHING SUGGESTIONS
- Model and encourage students to express the following process for comparing two jobs.
- Emphasize the wording commonly used to describe similarities. Repeat words that show similarity (both, and, like, similar, resemble, also, etc.) and encourage students to use them in their responses.
- Some Teachers reinforce students' responses by writing their comments on the HOW ARE TWO THINGS ALIKE diagram shown in the appendix. See the example at the right. Use a transparency or draw the diagram on chart paper or display board. Students begin to associate their answers with the words that they see on the diagram. However, if writing on the diagram distracts young children from thinking about the topic, using this method may not be helpful.

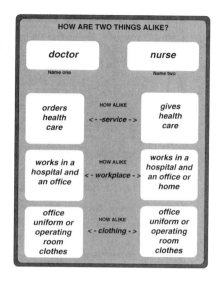

LESSON

Introduction
Teacher Comment: **In the last lesson we identified a job that was most like another.**

Stating the Objective
Teacher Comment: **In this lesson you will explain how certain jobs are alike.**

Conducting the Lesson
Teacher Comment: **Look at the top two jobs. Discuss with a partner how these two jobs are alike.**
  Student Response: Both help us keep our bodies healthy. They go to school for a long time to learn how all the parts of our bodies work, what healthy bodies need, and how to treat injuries or illnesses. They use special tools or medicines. Both wear special clothes and work in offices or hospitals.
Teacher Comment: **What did you describe to explain how these jobs are alike?**
  Student Response: I described how these health workers keep people healthy. I explained their training and the special tools or clothes they wear. I described where they work.
Teacher Comment: **Copy the words "doctor" and "nurse."**

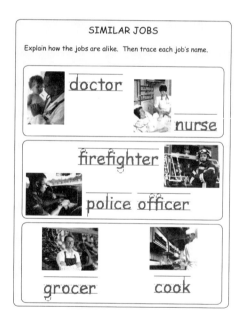

Teacher Comment: **Now look at the second pair of jobs. How are a police officer and a firefighter alike?**
  Student Response: Both work for the government. Both wear special uniforms. Both are sometimes in danger. Both help people stay safe.
Teacher Comment: **Copy the words "firefighter" and "police officer."**

Teacher Comment: **Look at the last pair of jobs. How are these jobs alike?**
  Student Response: Both buy and sell food. Both keep food safe and fresh.

Teacher Comment: **Trace the words "grocer" and "cook."**

Thinking About Thinking
Teacher Comment: **What did you explain about jobs to tell how they are alike?**
  Student Response:
  1. I explained their appearance, special equipment, special training, where they work, what they do.
  2. I explained how the two jobs are alike.
  3. I checked that I explained the important details of both jobs.

Personal Application
  Teacher Comment: **When is it important to tell how jobs are alike?**
    Student Response: I tell how jobs are alike to tell about jobs that are similar to ones I already understand; or to explain a job to someone who is unfamiliar with it.

Page 112 - SIMILARITIES AND DIFFERENCES

TEACHING SUGGESTIONS
- Emphasize the wording commonly used to describe similarities and differences. Repeat words that show similarity (both, and, like, similar, resemble, etc.) and encourage students to use them in their responses. Explain the term "unlike" and encourage students use words that cue differences (but, not, different, opposite, and unlike).
- Emphasize the difference between "comparing" (describing how two things are alike) and "contrasting" (explaining how two things are different). Correct mistaken usage of the terms and acknowledge students' correct use of these terms.
- To help young children express contrast, emphasize the use of the conjunction "but." Example: a grocer sells food, <u>but</u> a cook prepares food for customers. Explain that "but" is a signal word to alert the reader or listener that what comes after it will be different than what came before it. Encourage students to use this sentence pattern and acknowledge students' unprompted statements expressing contrast using this syntax.
- When contrasting jobs, students sometimes answer with a detail about only one of the jobs. For example, if the student answers that the barber cuts hair, confirm that it is correct that the barber cuts hair. Then ask whether the dentist cuts hair. The student then realizes that the dentist works on teeth. The student has now contrasted the part of the body that worker fixes.

LESSON

Introduction
  Teacher Comment: **We have described how jobs are alike. When we discuss how things are alike, we compare them. Sometimes we want to know how they are different in order to understand something important about them. When we describe how they are different, we contrast them.**

Stating the Objective
  Teacher Comment: **In this lesson you will explain how two jobs are alike and how they are different.**

Conducting the Lesson
  Teacher Comment: **How are the jobs of a barber and a dentist alike?**
    Student Response: Both must have special training, use special tools or supplies, and wear special clothes. Both help improve our appearance and cleanliness.
  Teacher Comment: **How are these jobs different?**
    Student Response: A barber uses scissors and clippers to cut hair, but the dentist uses special tools for working on the teeth. A barber learns to cut hair from other barbers or in special schools. A barber is not a doctor. A dentist is a doctor and goes to college for a long time to learn how treating teeth affects our whole body.
  Teacher Comment: **Trace the words "barber" and "dentist."**

  Teacher Comment: **Look at the next jobs. How are the jobs of a bus driver and a pilot alike?**
    Student Response: They both drive a large vehicle that carries passengers that pay for the ride. Both sit in the front of the vehicle and control its speed and direction.
  Teacher Comment: **How are these jobs different?**

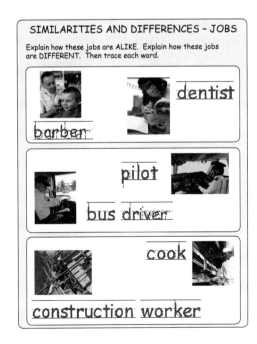

Student Response: The bus driver follows a land route and makes frequent stops to pick up and let off passengers. The pilot follows an air route and only stops at airports.
Teacher Comment: **Trace the words "pilot" and "bus driver."**

Teacher Comment: **Look at the next jobs. How are the jobs of a cook and a construction worker alike?**
Student Response: They both make something new. They both wear coverings over their clothes because they work with things that can stain them. Both use tools to make new things.
Teacher Comment: **How are these jobs different?**
Student Response: The cook quickly makes many different food items, but the construction worker works a long time on a large project. The cook's equipment is small and fits easily in a room. A construction worker's equipment sometimes includes tractors, cranes, or bulldozers that are huge vehicles. The cook works indoors and makes small things, but the construction worker works outside to build a huge building, highway, or bridge.
Teacher Comment: **Trace the words "cook" and "construction worker."**

Thinking About Thinking
Teacher Comment: **What did you explain about jobs to tell how they are alike or different?**
Student Response:
1. I explained their appearance, special equipment, where they work, what they do, special training.
2. I thought about similar details of the two jobs.
3. I thought about the different details in the two jobs.
4. I checked to see that I have identified the important details of both jobs.

Personal Application
Teacher Comment: **When is it important to understand how jobs are alike?**
Student Response: To suggest or recognize jobs that are similar to ones you already understand, to explain what friends or family members do for a living, to describe commercials, to describe services to a newcomer, thinking about the kind of job one might do as an adult, to explain a job to someone who is unfamiliar with it.

Page 113 - KINDS OF JOBS

TEACHING SUGGESTIONS

- Students will classify each occupation as either a producer or a service provider.
- Review the definitions of "goods" and "services" in your textbooks or see glossary at end of student book.

Introduction
Teacher Comment: **Some people make things that are sold or used by other people. The things that they make and sell are called "goods." Since they make goods, these jobs are "producers." What are some jobs that produce something that we buy or use.**
Student Response: Some producers are construction workers, farmers, and artists.
Teacher Comment: **Some workers are paid for doing something that people need. They provide a service. What are some jobs in which people are paid to do something for someone else?**
Student Response: Some service providers are teachers, firefighters, police officers, mail carriers, cooks, repairmen, restaurant servers, clerks in stores.

Stating the Objective
Teacher Comment: **In this lesson you will decide whether a job is a producer or provides a service.**

LESSON

Conducting the Lesson

Teacher Comment: **Name the occupation shown in the first picture.**
  Student Response: That person is an artist.
Teacher Comment: **What does an artist do?**
  Student Response: An artist paints a picture.
Teacher Comment: **Is the artist a producer or does she provide a service?**
  Student Response: Because she makes something that she sells, she is a producer.
Teacher Comment: **Notice the line from the artist to "producer." Trace and copy the word "producer."**

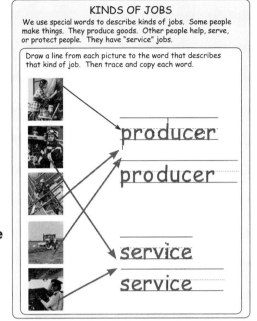

Teacher Comment: **Name the occupation in the second picture.**
  Student Response: That person is a firefighter.
Teacher Comment: **What does a firefighter do?**
  Student Response: A firefighter helps you protect your home from fire or puts out a fire if one should happen.
Teacher Comment: **Is the firefighter a producer or does he provide a service?**
  Student Response: The firefighter provides a service.
Teacher Comment: **Draw a line from the firefighter to the word "service." Trace and copy the word "service."**

Teacher Comment: **Name the occupation in the third picture.**
  Student Response: That person is a construction worker.
Teacher Comment: **What does a construction worker do?**
  Student Response: A construction worker builds things. He is a producer.
Teacher Comment: **Draw a line from the picture to the word "producer."**

Teacher Comment: **Name the occupation in the fourth picture.**
  Student Response: That person is a farmer.
Teacher Comment: **What does a farmer do?**
  Student Response: A farmer raises food. He is a producer.
Teacher Comment: **Draw a line from the picture to the word "producer."**

Teacher Comment: **Name the occupation in the last picture.**
  Student Response: That person is a pilot.
Teacher Comment: **What does a pilot do?**
  Student Response: A pilot flies an airplane or a helicopter for passengers. A pilot does a service.
Teacher Comment: **Draw a line from the picture to the word "service."**

Thinking About Thinking

Teacher Comment: **What did you think about to decide what kind of job is shown the picture?**
  Student Response:
  1. I looked at each picture and identified the job.
  2. I remembered the important details about that job (whether a worker is a makes something or is paid to do something for other people).
  3. I looked for the word for that kind of job.

Personal Application

Teacher Comment: **When is it important to understand whether a job is a producer or does a service?**
  Student Response: I need to know whether a job is a producer or does a service to understand how a person is paid.

Page 114 - KINDS OF JOBS

TEACHING ABOUT JOBS

Introduction
   Teacher Comment: We have learned that some workers are paid for doing something that other people need. They provide a service.
   In this lesson you will learn about different kinds of service providers. The people that you call to keep you safe are "emergency workers." The people that help you stay well or help you heal when you are sick or injured are "health care workers." People who do something for you are "service providers."

Stating the Objective
   Teacher Comment: In this lesson you will decide whether a person is an emergency worker, a health care worker, or a service provider.

LESSON

Conducting the Lesson

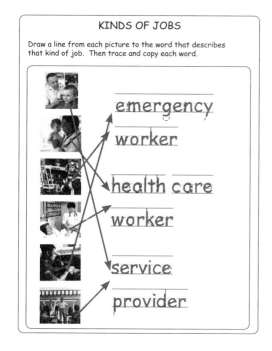

   Teacher Comment: **Name the worker shown in the first picture.**
      Student Response: The worker is a barber.
   Teacher Comment: **What does the barber do?**
      Student response: The barber cuts hair.
   Teacher Comment: **Is the barber an emergency worker, a health care worker, or a service provider?**
      Student Response: The barber is paid to help people look good. He is a service provider.
   Teacher Comment: **Draw a line from the barber to "service provider." Trace the words "service provider."**

   Teacher Comment: **Name the worker shown in the second picture.**
      Student Response: The worker is a doctor.
   Teacher Comment: **What does a doctor do?**
      Student Response: A doctor helps us to stay well and to heal if we are sick or injured.
   Teacher Comment: **Is a doctor an emergency worker, a health care worker, or a service provider?**
      Student Response: He is a health care worker.
   Teacher Comment: **Draw a line from the picture of the doctor to the words "health care worker." Trace the words "health care worker."**

   Teacher Comment: **Name the worker shown in the third picture.**
      Student Response: The worker is a firefighter.
   Teacher Comment: **What does a firefighter do?**
      Student Response: A firefighter puts out fires.
   Teacher Comment: **Is a firefighter an emergency worker, a health care worker, or a service provider?**
      Student Response: A firefighter is an emergency worker.
   Teacher Comment: **Draw a line from the picture of the firefighter to the words "emergency worker."**

- Continue this dialog for nurse, police officer, and teacher.

Thinking About Thinking
   Teacher Comment: **What did you think about to decide what kind of job is shown the picture?**
   Student Response:
     1. I looked at each picture and identified the job.
     2. I remembered the important details about that job and decided whether a worker is an emergency worker, a health care worker, or a service provider.
     3. I looked for the words for that kind of job.

Personal Application
   Teacher Comment: **When is it important to understand whether a job is an emergency worker, a health care worker, or a service provider?**
   Student Response: I need to know what kind of service a worker provides to understand how important that job is to the community and to tell or write about it.

CHAPTER TEN – THINKING ABOUT VEHICLES (Pages 116-130)

TEACHING ABOUT VEHICLES

CURRICULUM APPLICATIONS
Social Studies: Identify how a family depends upon transportation to meet its needs; identify some jobs in the home, school, and community; cite examples of community needs and services; understand how community helpers are an example of interdependence

LANGUAGE INTEGRATION ACTIVITIES

- A list of vehicles described in this chapter is provided in the appendix. To help students associate the word with the picture of the vehicle, enlarge this list for display and refer to the term for various vehicles as you teach the lesson.

- Drawing: Ask students to draw a picture of a vehicle. Students may write or give short descriptions of the vehicle. Create a vehicle bulletin board display of students' drawings.

- Listening: Prior to a lesson that features a vehicle, read aloud a non-fiction picture book about that vehicle. Language experiences with the book extends this lesson and demonstrates how various vehicles meet individual family needs. After discussing the picture books ask the following questions:
  Are there any new ideas about (any vehicle) that we learned from this story?
  What ideas or details about (any vehicle) did you learn from the pictures?

- Select a common story or fairy tale about vehicles, such as *Little Toot* by Hardie Gramatky. Ask students to retell the story about another vehicle (e.g. a tractor instead of tug boat). Discuss how the revised story is different from the original. For example the tractor would face different land obstacles, such as mud or snow instead of stormy seas or fog.

  After discussing each story, ask students to add new information about the characteristics of the various vehicles described in the story to the lists, posters, or graphic organizers that you may have used when discussing the pictures.

TEACHING SUGGESTIONS

- "Vehicles" or "public transportation" are abstract concepts for most young children. Since they have heard these terms several times in previous exercises, students should begin to use them independently.

MENTAL MODEL
A mental model is a framework for understanding a concept. It outlines the characteristics that one must state to describe or define a concept. After completing this chapter, each kindergarten student will have applied this mental model to vehicles in the lessons. A mental model helps a student:

- Anticipate what he or she needs to know to understand a new vehicle
- Remember the characteristics of a vehicle
- State a clear definition or write an adequate description of a vehicle
- Explain a vehicle to someone else

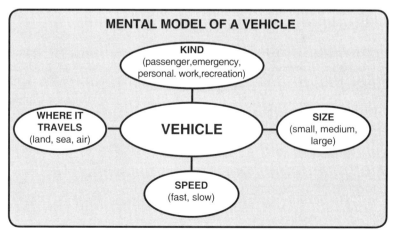

Kindergarten Thinking Skills & Key Concepts   Teacher's Manual

Page 116 - DESCRIBING VEHICLES

- Students may not know terms for public transportation. "Route," "fare," and "schedule" are introduced in this lesson. Encourage students to use these words when discussing public vehicles.

LESSON
Introduction
  Teacher Comment: **When we studied different jobs, we learned that many workers need special vehicles. Family members use vehicles to get to work and to shop for what they need. As we discuss different vehicles, we will learn why they are important to families and communities.**

Stating the Objective
  Teacher Comment: **In this lesson you will listen to information about a vehicle and select the one that fits the description.**

Conducting the Lesson
  Teacher Comment: **I will describe one of the vehicles. Select the picture that fits the description. This vehicle has emergency equipment, and carries sick or injured people to the hospital. It contains medicine, tables for moving people, and bandages. Emergency workers use its machines to help doctors understand what the patient needs and to keep people safe on the trip to the hospital. It can go fast in traffic because flashing lights and sirens warn people to get out of the way. It doesn't stop for signs or lights on its trip to the hospital. What do we call this vehicle?**
  Student Response: That vehicle is an ambulance.
  Teacher Comment: **Circle the picture of the ambulance.**

  Teacher Comment: **What clues let you know that the vehicle that was described was an ambulance?**
  Student Response: The square shape allows room in the rear for a patient, the equipment, and emergency workers. The lights, siren, and the markings tell drivers that it is an emergency vehicle that will not stop for traffic signals.
  Teacher Comment: **Why don't the other vehicles fit the description?**
  Student Response: A police car has lights and sirens, but does not look like a truck and has no room for a patient to lay down. A truck is not an emergency vehicle that will not stop for traffic signals.

  Teacher Comment: **Look at the second row of vehicles. This vehicle is much larger than a car and carries lots of people. It travels a regular route on the same streets around the city or from one city to another. Passengers read signs or lists to know its schedule - the route that it travels at the same time every day. The money that people pay to ride on it is called a fare. Because of its large size and its many stops, traveling on it takes longer than riding in a car. What do we call this vehicle?**
  Student Response: That vehicle is a bus.
  Teacher Comment: **Circle the picture of the bus.**

  Teacher Comment: **What clues let you know that the vehicle that was described was a bus?**
  Student Response: Its size, speed, where it travels, and that passengers pay to use it, show that it is a bus.
  Teacher Comment: **Why don't the other vehicles fit the description?**
  Student Response: Airplanes do not run on streets. Tractors do not carry passengers.

  Teacher Comment: **Look at the third row of vehicles. Select the picture that fits the following description. This vehicle has two wheels and handle bars. The driver pedals it to make it go. It is usually ridden by only one person. Children often ride to school on one. It travels faster than walking, but slower than a car. What do we call this vehicle?**
  Student Response: That vehicle is a bicycle.
  Teacher Comment: **Circle the picture of the bicycle.**

Teacher Comment: **What clues let you know that the vehicle that was described was a bicycle?**
  Student Response: The number of wheels, its parts, who rides it, and how it moves show that this vehicle is a bicycle.
Teacher Comment: **Why don't the other vehicles fit the description?**
  Student Response: The other vehicles are run by a motor and cannot be driven by children.

Thinking About Thinking:
  Teacher Comment: **What details did you look for when you picked out the vehicle that was described?**
  Student Response:
    1. I listened for the important details of the vehicle (its size, speed, where it travels, who uses it, how it moves).
    2. I found the important details in the pictures.
    3. I checked that the pictures of other vehicles do not show those important details.

Personal Application
  Teacher Comment: **When is it important to describe vehicles accurately?**
  Student Response: I must describe vehicles to describe deliveries, to describe traffic, or to give directions.

Page 117 - DESCRIBING VEHICLES

TEACHING SUGGESTIONS
- Although boats are generally smaller than ships, it may not be useful to make this distinction. Use common terms such as ferry boat.
- Students may not commonly use the term "vehicle." Explain that a vehicle is propelled by an engine within it, such as a car or airplane, or by some force that is applied to it, such as a person pedaling or wind pushing sails.
- Students may not commonly use the term transportation. Explain that transportation means moving people or things from one place to another.
- Because many students may not know how a helicopter works and what it is used for, read and discuss a picture book about helicopters prior to this lesson.

LESSON

Introduction
  Teacher Comment: **We have selected a vehicle from its description.**

Stating the Objective
  Teacher Comment: **In this lesson you will describe vehicles. Look at the first picture. Name this vehicle and describe it to your partner.**

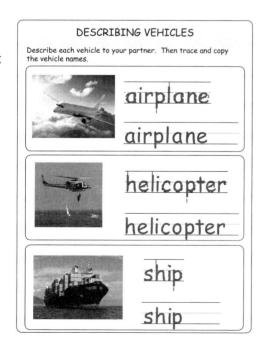

  Student Response: An airplane is a large vehicle that flies very fast in the air. It has a large engine, wings, and can fly long distances. It carries passengers who pay a fare to ride on it. Because it flies to different cities every day, passengers must find out its schedule to buy their tickets.
  Teacher Comment: **Trace and write the word "airplane" in the lined spaces.**

  Teacher Comment: **What details do you describe to explain that the vehicle in the picture is an airplane?**
  Student Response: I described its size, that it travels in the air, and that it carries passengers.

  Teacher Comment: **The second picture shows a vehicle that has rotors. A rotor is similar to a propeller. It turns very fast, blowing air to make the vehicle move. One rotor makes it move up and down. The other rotor makes it turn. Name this vehicle and describe it to your partner.**

Student Response: A helicopter flies straight up, down, or forward in the air. It can land in very small places. It has large blades that spin quickly to make it move. A helicopter can carry one to twelve people. It travels fast to rescue people at sea or to get accident victims to help quickly by flying over traffic.
Teacher Comment: **Trace and copy the word "helicopter" on the lines.**

Teacher Comment: **What details do you describe to explain that the vehicle in the picture is a helicopter?**
Student Response: I described how the rotors make it move fast through the air. I told how it is used.

Teacher Comment: **Look at the third vehicle. Name this vehicle and describe it to your partner.**
Student Response: A ship is a very large boat that carries people and things long distances over the ocean. Some ships carry large numbers of people. Some ships carry large loads, such as cars or oil. Some ships are used by the navy for defense, such as aircraft carriers. Ships have huge engines that turn large propellers that push them slowly through the water.
Teacher Comment: **Trace and write the word "ship" in the lined spaces.**

Teacher Comment: **What details do you describe to explain that the vehicle in the picture is a ship?**
Student Response: I described the ship's size, that it travels over the water, and that it carries people and large loads.

Thinking About Thinking
Teacher Comment: **What did you think about when you described vehicles?**
Student Response:
1. I recalled the important details of the vehicle (its size, its speed, whether it travels on land, water, or in the air, and how it moves).
2. I checked that I described all those important details.
3. I checked that I had given enough details to keep the vehicle I am describing from being confused with other kinds of vehicles.

Personal Application
Teacher Comment: **When is it important to describe vehicles accurately?**
Student Response: I need to describe vehicles to describe deliveries, to describe traffic, or to give directions.

Page 118 - NAMING VEHICLES

LESSON

Introduction
Teacher Comment: **We have described vehicles.**

Stating the Objective
Teacher Comment: **In this lesson you will match vehicles to their names**

Conducting the lesson
Teacher Comment: **The first picture shows a police car. Notice that an arrow is drawn from the picture of police car to the words "police car." Trace and copy the words "police car."**

Teacher Comment: **Name the vehicle shown in the second picture.**
Student Response: The second picture shows a ship.
Teacher Comment: **Draw a line from the picture of the ship to the word "ship." Trace and copy the word "ship."**

- Continue this dialog to discuss the remaining pictures.

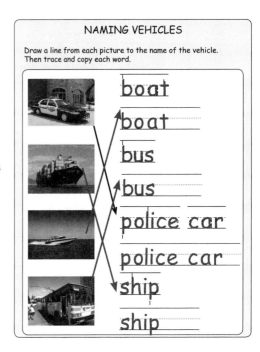

Thinking About Thinking
　　Teacher Comment: **How did you decide which word belonged with each picture?**
　　Student Response:
　　　1. I looked at the details of the vehicle in the picture.
　　　2. I named that vehicle.
　　　3. I found the word for that vehicle.

Personal Application
　　Teacher Comment: **When is it important to understand how to name vehicles?**
　　Student Response: I need to know how to write about them or to give directions.

Page 119 - CHARACTERISTICS OF VEHICLES

LESSON

Introduction
　　Teacher Comment: **We describe a vehicle as small, medium, or large compared to other vehicles.**

Stating the Objective
　　Teacher Comment: **In this lesson you will describe vehicles by their size.**

Conducting the Lesson
　　Teacher Comment: **Name the vehicles in the first box.**
　　　Student Response: The vehicles are a pickup truck, a motorcycle, and a train.
　　Teacher Comment: **The pictures make the vehicles look like they are the same size. Look at the surroundings and what you know about the vehicles to decide its size.**
　　Teacher Comment: **Which vehicle is small?**
　　　Student Response: The motorcycle is small.
　　Teacher Comment: **Draw a line from the motorcycle to the word "small" and trace the word "small."**

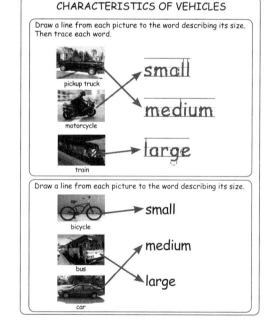

　　Teacher Comment: **Which vehicle is large?**
　　　Student Response: The train is large.
　　Teacher Comment: **Draw a line from the train to the word "large" and trace the word "large."**

　　Teacher Comment: **Which vehicle is medium in size?**
　　　Student Response: The pickup truck is medium in size.
　　Teacher Comment: **Draw a line from the pickup truck to the word "medium" and trace the word "medium.**

　　Teacher Comment: **In the bottom box draw a line from each picture to the word describing its size.**

Thinking About Thinking
　　Teacher Comment: **What did you think about to describe the size of vehicles.**
　　Student Response:
　　　1. I remembered the size of the vehicle and what I saw in the picture.
　　　2. I thought about how big it is compared to other vehicles.
　　　3. I described it as small, medium, or large.

Personal Application
　　Teacher Comment: **When is it important to describe the size of a vehicle?**
　　　Student Response: I need to describe the size of a vehicle when I write a story about it or compare it to others.

PAGE 120 - DESCRIBING VEHICLES

LESSON

- Young children understand the meaning of "fast" and "slow," though they may not use the term "speed" to describe motion. Encourage students to use "speed" to describe this property.

Introduction
Teacher Comment: **We have learned to describe vehicles by their size. We also describe vehicles by their speed. Some vehicles move fast and some move slowly.**

Stating the Objective
Teacher Comment: **In this lesson you will match the picture of each vehicle to the two words that describe both its size and its speed.**

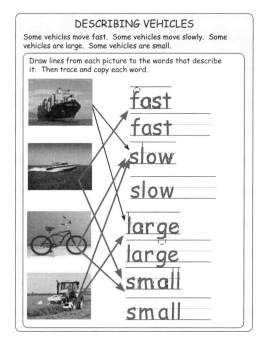

Conducting the Lesson
Teacher Comment: **Name the vehicle in the top picture.**
 Student Response: The first vehicle is a ship.
Teacher Comment: **A ship is a large vehicle, larger than a motorboat. Notice that a line is drawn from the ship to the word "large." Trace and copy the word "large."**

Teacher Comment: **A large ship moves slowly. Notice that a line is drawn from the ship to the word "slow." Trace and copy the word "slow."**

Teacher Comment: **The second picture shows a motorboat. Is a motorboat large or small compared to other boats or ships?**
 Student Response: A motorboat is small.
Teacher Comment: **Draw a line from the picture of the motorboat to the word "small." Trace and copy the word "small."**

Teacher Comment: **Which word describes the speed of a small motorboat - fast or slow?**
 Student Response: "Fast" describes the speed of a small motorboat.
Teacher Comment: **Draw a line from the motorboat to the word "fast." Trace and copy the word "fast."**

Teacher Comment: **Name the vehicle in the third picture.**
 Student Response: That vehicle is a bicycle.
Teacher Comment: **Is a bicycle small or large?**
 Student Response: A bicycle is a small vehicle.
Teacher Comment: **Draw a line from bicycle to the word "small."**

Teacher Comment: **Is a bicycle fast or slow compared to other vehicles on the road?**
 Student Response: A bicycle is a slow vehicle.
Teacher Comment: **Draw a line from the bicycle to the word "slow."**

- Continue this dialog for tractor.

Thinking About Thinking
Teacher Comment: **How did you decide which word belonged with each picture?**
 Student Response:
 1. I looked at each picture and identified the vehicle.
 2. I looked at its size compared to its surroundings and remembered what I know about the vehicle.
 3. I thought about its size and speed compared to other vehicles.
 4. I found the words that describe the size and speed of the vehicle.

Personal Application
Teacher Comment: **When is it important to describe a vehicle?**
 Student Response: I need to describe a vehicle when I write a story or tell my friends about one.

Page 121 - DESCRIBING PARTS OF A BICYCLE

LESSON

Introduction
   Teacher Comment: **To describe vehicles we sometimes need to know the names of its parts and explain how each part is important for the vehicle to work properly.**

Stating the Objective
   Teacher Comment: **In this lesson you will think about the parts of a bicycle, what that part does, and what would happen if that part was missing or damaged.**

Conducting the Lesson
   Teacher Comment: **Which part steers the bike?**
      Student Response: The handlebars steer the bike.
   Teacher Comment: **Use the words in the WORD BOX to write the word "handlebars" on the blank lines in the top box.**

   Teacher Comment: **What would happen if the handlebars were missing or damaged?**
      Student Response: The rider couldn't steer the bike.

   Teacher Comment: **Look at the second box. This part holds the rider. What is it called?**
      Student Response: The part that holds the rider is the seat.
   Teacher Comment: **Write the word "seat" on the blank lines in the second box.**

   Teacher Comment: **What would happen if the seat was missing or damaged?**
      Student Response: The rider could not sit down.

   Teacher Comment: **Look at the third box. This part rolls so the bike can move. What is it called?**
      Student Response: The part that rolls is the wheel.
   Teacher Comment: **Write the word "wheel" on the blank lines in the third box.**

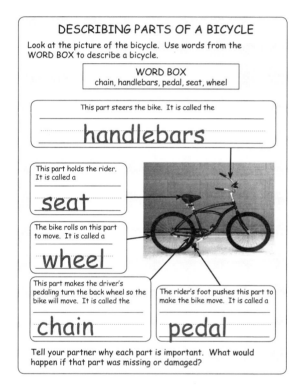

   Teacher Comment: **What would happen if the wheel was missing or damaged?**
      Student Response: The bike could not roll.

   Teacher Comment: **Look at the fourth box. This part turns the back wheel when the rider pedals so the bike will move. What is it called?**
      Student Response: The part that makes the back wheel turn is the chain.
   Teacher Comment: **Write the word "chain" on the blank lines in the fourth box.**

   Teacher Comment: **What would happen if the chain was missing or damaged?**
      Student Response: The back wheel would not turn.

   Teacher Comment: **Look at the last box. The rider's foot pushes on this part to make the bike move. What is it called?**
      Student Response: The part that the rider's foot pushes on is the pedal.
   Teacher Comment: **Write the word "pedal" on the blank lines in the fourth box.**

   Teacher Comment: **What would happen if the pedal was missing or damaged?**
      Student Response: The driver could not make the back wheel turn to make the bicycle move.

Thinking About Thinking
   Teacher Comment: **What did you think about in order to describe the parts of a bicycle?**
   Student Response:
   1. I named the part.
   2. I remembered what it is used for.
   3. I thought about what would happen if that part was missing.

Personal Application
   Teacher Comment: **When is it important to describe parts of a whole vehicle?**
   Student Response: I describe the parts of a vehicle to explain how it works and how it is different from other vehicles. I describe the parts to tell a story about a vehicle.

Page 122 - DESCRIBING PARTS OF A FIRE TRUCK

- Young children may not know that "warning signal" refers to the lights and siren of an emergency vehicle. They may not know that "cab" refers to the space where the driver sits on a tractor or fire truck. Discuss a picture book about a fire truck to introduce these terms before conducting the lesson.

LESSON

Introduction
   Teacher Comment: **In the last lesson we described the parts of a bicycle.**

Stating the Objective
   Teacher Comment: **In this lesson you will think about the parts of a fire truck, what that part does, and what would happen if that part was missing.**

Conducting the Lesson
   Teacher Comment: **Which part of the fire truck has lights and makes loud sounds to tell drivers to let it pass?**
   Student Response: The warning signal tells drivers to let it pass.
   Teacher Comment: **Use the words from the WORD BOX to write the word "warning signal" on the blank lines in the top box.**

   Teacher Comment: **What would happen if the warning signal was missing?**
   Student Response: The fire truck might not be seen by drivers. They would not move over to let the fire truck get to a fire quickly. Not seeing the fire truck might cause an accident.

   Teacher Comment: **Look at the second box. Which part is used by firefighters to reach high places?**
   Student Response: The ladder helps firefighters reach high places.
   Teacher Comment: **Write the word "ladder" on the blank lines in the second box.**

   Teacher Comment: **What would happen if the ladder was missing?**
   Student Response: The firefighters would not be able to put out the fire or rescue people high up in the building.

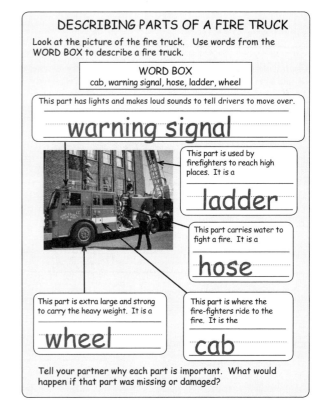

Teacher Comment: **Look at the third box. Which part carries water to fight a fire?**
Student Response: The hose carries water to fight a fire.
Teacher Comment: **Write the word "hose" on the blank lines in the third box.**

Teacher Comment: **What would happen if the hose was missing?**
Student Response: The firefighters would not have water to put out the fire.

Teacher Comment: **Look at the box on the bottom left. Which part is extra large and strong to carry the weight of the fire truck?**
Student Response: The wheel is extra large and strong.
Teacher Comment: **Write the word "wheel" on the blank lines in the third box.**

Teacher Comment: **What would happen if the wheel was missing?**
Student Response: The fire truck could not move.

Teacher Comment: **Look at the last box. Where do the firefighters ride .**
Student Response: The firefighters ride in the cab.
Teacher Comment: **Write the word "cab" on the blank lines in the third box.**

Teacher Comment: **What would happen if the cab was missing?**
Student Response: The fire truck would not carry enough firefighters to put out the fire.

Thinking About Thinking
Teacher Comment: **What did you think about in order to describe the parts of a fire truck?**
Student Response:
1. I named the part.
2. I remembered what it is used for.
3. I thought about what would happen if that part was missing.

Personal Application
Teacher Comment: **When is it important to describe parts of a vehicle?**
Student Response: I describe the parts of a vehicle to explain how it works and how it is different from other vehicles. I describe the parts to tell a story about a vehicle.

Page 123 - SIMILAR VEHICLES

TEACHING SUGGESTIONS
- Emphasize the wording commonly used to describe similarities. Repeat words that show similarity (both, and, like, similar, resemble, also, etc.) and encourage students to use them in their responses.
- Young students may not realize that generally a ship is any large boat. However, trying to distinguish between a ship and a boat is probably not useful, since the term "boat" may sometimes apply to a large vessel, such as a fishing boat or a ferry boat.
- Some teachers reinforce students' responses by writing their comments on the HOW ARE TWO THINGS ALIKE diagram shown in the appendix. See the example at the right. Use a transparency or draw the diagram on chart paper or display board. Students begin to associate their answers with the words that they see on the diagram. However, if writing on the diagram distracts young children from thinking about the topic, using this method may not be helpful.

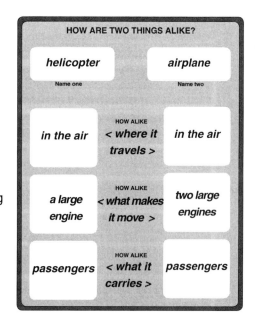

LESSON

Introduction
 Teacher Comment: **We have practiced describing many vehicles.**

Stating the Objective
 Teacher Comment: **In this lesson you will look at a picture of a vehicle and then decide which of three vehicles is most like it.**

Conducting the Lesson
 Teacher Comment: **Name the vehicles in the example.**
  Student Response: The vehicles are an ambulance, a car, a fire truck, and a pickup truck.
 Teacher Comment: **Tell your partner all the important things that you know about an ambulance.**
  Student Response: An ambulance is a vehicle that is used to bring a very sick or injured person to the hospital. It contains special equipment and medical supplies that help keep a person alive on the trip. It is equipped with a siren and flashing lights that let people know it is going to an emergency or to the hospital.
 Teacher Comment: **Which vehicle at the right is most like an ambulance?**
  Student Response: A fire truck is a vehicle that carries ladders and other equipment or tools a firefighter uses to fight and put out fires. Fire trucks have lights and sirens that let people know when they are going to a fire. This vehicle is used during an emergency or when people are in danger and need help.
 Teacher Comment: **Notice that a circle is drawn around the fire truck.**
 Teacher Comment: **What clues let you know that a fire truck is most like an ambulance?**
  Student Response: Both are emergency vehicles which have sirens and equipment to help people who are in danger.
 Teacher Comment: **How are the other vehicles different from an ambulance?**
  Student Response: The car and pickup truck are not emergency vehicles with sirens. They are used to carry people or large objects.

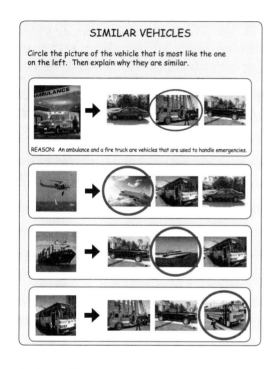

 Teacher Comment: **Name the vehicles shown in the second row.**
  Student Response: The vehicles are a helicopter, an airplane, a bus, and a car.
 Teacher Comment: **Tell your partner all the important things that you know about a helicopter.**
  Student Response: A helicopter flies straight up and down or across in the air. It can land in very small places. It has large blades that spin quickly to give it speed to rise into the air. A helicopter can only carry a few people.
 Teacher Comment: **Which vehicle on the right is most like a helicopter?**
  Student Response: An airplane is a vehicle that can fly. It has two wings and one or more engines that turn propellers. Airplanes can carry people, packages, and other things from one place to another.
 Teacher Comment: **Draw a circle around the picture of the airplane.**

 Teacher Comment: **What clues let you know that a helicopter is most like an airplane?**
  Student Response: Both fly and can carry passengers through the air.
 Teacher Comment: **How are the other vehicles different from a helicopter?**
  Student Response: A bus and a car travel along the ground and cannot fly.

 Teacher Comment: **Look at the third row. Name the vehicles.**
  Student Response: The vehicles are a ship, a pickup truck, a motorboat, and a bus.

Teacher Comment: **Tell your partner all the important things that you know about a ship.**
Student Response: A ship is a large boat that carries people and loads long distances. Some ships, like ocean liners, carry large numbers of people and are like a large floating hotel. Some carry freight, like cars or oil. Some are used by the military for defense, such as aircraft carriers. Ships have huge engines that turn huge propellers that push the ship through the water.
Teacher Comment: **Which vehicle on the right is most like a ship?**
Student Response: A motorboat is most like a ship. It has a motor and travels on water.
Teacher Comment: **Draw a circle around the picture of the motorboat.**

Teacher Comment: **What clues let you know that a ship is most like a boat?**
Student Response: Both travel on water and carry people. Both have motors.
Teacher Comment: **How are the other vehicles different from a ship?**
Student Response: A truck or a bus cannot float.

- Continue this dialog to discuss the vehicles in the last row: bus, fire truck, pickup truck, and school bus.

Thinking About Thinking
Teacher Comment: **What did you think about to decide which vehicle is most like another one?**
Student Response:
1. I recalled the important details of the first vehicle (its size, its speed, how it moves, whether it travels on land, sea, or in the air, appearance, special equipment, etc.).
2. I looked for similar details in the other vehicles.
3. I selected the vehicle that has most of the same details.
4. I checked to see that other vehicles do not fit the important details.

Personal Application
Teacher Comment: **When is it important to understand how two vehicles are alike?**
Student Response: I need to understand how two vehicles are alike to describe deliveries or traffic, or to tell how these vehicles are used.

Page 124 - SIMILAR VEHICLES

TEACHING SUGGESTIONS
- Emphasize the wording commonly used to describe similarities. Repeat words that show similarity (both, and, like, similar, resemble, also, etc.) and encourage students to use them in their responses.
- Some teachers reinforce students' responses by writing their comments on the HOW ARE TWO THINGS ALIKE diagram (shown to the right and included in the appendix). Use a transparency or draw the diagram on chart paper or display board. See the example on the right. Students begin to associate their answers with the words that they see on the diagram. However, if writing on the diagram distracts young children from thinking about the topic, using this method may not be helpful.

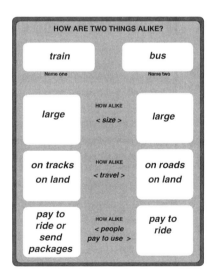

LESSON

Introduction
Teacher Comment: **We have practiced identifying similar vehicles.**

Stating the Objective
Teacher Comment: **In this lesson you will explain how two vehicles are alike.**

Conducting the Lesson
Teacher Comment: **The top row shows a train and a bus. Explain how these vehicles are alike.**

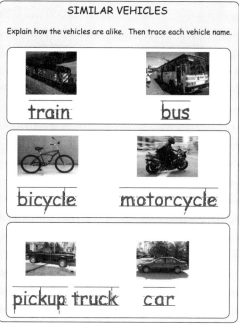

Student Response: Both are large vehicles that can carry many passengers. Both are powered by large engines. Many buses and trains have long routes between cities. Both have schedules that tell when and where they will arrive. Passengers pay a fare and know its schedule to ride on them.
Teacher Comment: **Trace the words "train" and "bus."**

Teacher Comment: **The second row shows a bicycle and a motorcycle. Explain how these vehicles are alike.**
Student Response: Both are small two-wheeled vehicles that have handlebars for steering and a seat for the driver. They can safely carry one person. Both are small and can maneuver in traffic. They use little or no fuel. They are both open vehicles with no covering to protect the driver from rain or injury. They cannot carry large loads.
Teacher Comment: **Trace the words "bicycle" and "motorcycle."**

Teacher Comment: **The last row shows a pickup truck and a car. How are these vehicles are alike?**
Student Response: Both are passenger vehicles. They have four wheels and two or four doors. People often drive them to work or school and to run errands.
Teacher Comment: **Trace the words "pickup truck" and "car."**

- Continue this dialog for school bus and bus.

Thinking About Thinking
Teacher Comment: **What did you explain about vehicles to tell how they are alike?**
Student Response:
1. I explained its appearance, special equipment, its size, its speed, whether is travels on land, sea, or in the air, who uses it, and what it is used for.
2. I looked for details that both vehicles have.
3. I checked that I explained the important details of both vehicles.

Personal Application
Teacher Comment: **When is it important to understand how two vehicles are alike?**
Student Response: I need to understand how two vehicles are alike to describe deliveries or traffic, or to tell how these vehicles are used.

Page 125 - SIMILARITIES AND DIFFERENCES

- Emphasize the difference between "comparing" (describing how two things are alike) and "contrasting" (explaining how two things are different). Correct mistaken usage of the terms and acknowledge students' correct use of these terms.

- Emphasize the wording commonly used to describe similarities and differences. Repeat words that show similarity (both, and, like, similar, resemble, also, etc.) and encourage students to use them in their responses. Explain the term "unlike" and encourage students use words that cue differences (but, not, different, opposite, and unlike).

- To help young children express contrast, emphasize the use of the conjunction "but." For example: The bus travels on land, but the airplane travels in the air.

- Young children will observe color before other more subtle characteristics. If a child explains that the train is green and the plane is white, confirm that the difference in color is true for the vehicles pictured in the exercise. Ask whether all trains are green and all airplanes white. When the child realizes that color is not a defining characteristic for vehicles, confirm again that color is not a characteristic that distinguishes one type of vehicle from another. Note: A school bus is an example of a vehicle for which color can be a defining characteristic, since public school buses are almost always yellow.

- When contrasting vehicles students sometimes answer with a detail about only one of the vehicles. For example, if the student answers that the airplane has wings, confirm that it is correct that the plane has wings to help it get into the air. Then ask whether the train has wings. The student then realizes that the long, thin shape of the train is different from the wide wings of the airplane.

- The student's response about "wings" also leads to a second difference - where it travels. The train does not need wings because it moves on a track on the ground. The full answer then becomes that the airplane has wings so that it can travel in the air, but the train does not have wings because it travels on the ground.

LESSON

Introduction
  Teacher Comment: **In the last lesson we explained how two vehicles were alike.**

Stating the Objective
  Teacher Comment: **In this lesson you will explain how two vehicles are alike and how they are different.**

Conducting the Lesson
  Teacher Comment: **The first row shows a train and an airplane. How are these vehicles alike?**
    Student Response: Both are vehicles used to move people from one place to another over long distances. People pay a fare to ride on them. They usually follow schedules and make regular stops on a route. Special planes or trains carry only freight.
  Teacher Comment: **How are these vehicles different?**
    Student Response: The train travels on land, but the airplane travels in the air.
  Teacher Comment: **Trace the words "train" and "airplane."**

  Teacher Comment: **What did you discuss to explain how these vehicles are alike or different?**
    Student Response: I thought about its size, what it is used for, how it is propelled (both require large engines), and when it is used.

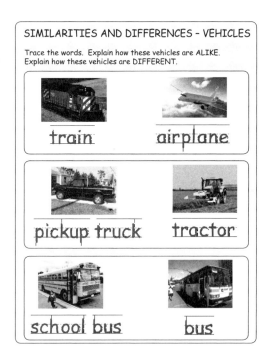

Teacher Comment: **The second row shows a pickup truck and a tractor. How are these vehicles alike?**
Student Response: Both are used on farms and are powered by large engines. They can be used to pull wagons and other equipment.
Teacher Comment: **How are these vehicles different?**
Student Response: The pickup truck often travels on roads and highways. Some people use a pickup truck like a car for errands and going to work. The tractor stays mainly on the farm and only occasionally goes on the road.
Teacher Comment: **Trace the words "pickup truck" and "tractor."**

Teacher Comment: **What did you discuss to explain how these vehicles are alike or different?**
Student Response: I thought about its size, what it is used for, where it is driven, that they are owned by individuals, and when it is used.

Teacher Comment: **The last row shows a school bus and a city bus. How are these vehicles alike?**
Student Response: Both are vehicles used to move many people from one place to another. Usually large, they come in different sizes. They have a similar shape. They both have rows of seats and windows so that the passengers can look out. They both travel the same route each day. They both have a schedule to pickup passengers.
Teacher Comment: **How are these vehicles different?**
Student Response: Any passenger can ride a bus, but only students ride a school bus. Passengers pay a fare to ride a bus, but students do not pay to ride a school bus. Passengers can get off the bus at any stop that they choose, but students only get off the school bus at school or their bus stop. Buses are many different colors, but school buses are usually yellow.
Teacher Comment: **What did you discuss to explain how these vehicles are alike or different?**
Student Response: I thought about its size, who rides on it, whether people pay a fare to ride, what it is used for, its appearance, where it is driven, when it is used, and its regular route

Thinking About Thinking
Teacher Comment: **What did you explain about vehicles to tell how they are alike or different?**
Student Response:
1. I explained their appearance, special equipment, size, speed, whether they travel on land, sea, or in the air, who uses them, and what they are used for.
2. I explained similar details of the two vehicles
3. I explained the different details of the two vehicles.
4. I checked that I have explained the important details of both vehicles.

Personal Application
Teacher Comment: **When is it important to tell how vehicles are alike or different?**
Student Response: I need to describe vehicles to describe deliveries; to describe traffic; or to give directions.

Kindergarten Thinking Skills & Key Concepts — Teacher's Manual

Pages 126 - KINDS OF VEHICLES

LESSON

Introduction
    Teacher Comment: **Some vehicles travel on the land, others travel by sea. Some vehicles fly in the air.**

Explaining the Objective to Students
    Teacher Comment: **In this lesson you will match vehicles to the group in which it belongs.**

Conducting the Lesson
    Teacher Comment: **Name the first vehicle.**
      Student Response: It is a motorboat.
    Teacher Comment: **Does the motorboat travel on land, sea, or air?**
      Student Response: The motor boat travels on water.
    Teacher Comment: **Draw a line from the photograph to the words "sea vehicles."**

    Teacher Comment: **Trace and copy the words "sea vehicles."**

    Teacher Comment: **Name the second vehicle.**
      Student Response: The second vehicle is a helicopter.
    Teacher Comment: **Vehicles that travel in the air are called air vehicles. Draw lines from the photograph to "air vehicles." Trace and copy the words "air vehicles."**
    Teacher Comment: **Name the third vehicle.**
      Student Response: The third vehicle is a train.
    Teacher Comment: **Vehicles that travel on the land are called land vehicles. Draw lines from the photograph to the words "land vehicles." Trace and copy the words "land vehicles."**

- Continue the dialog for airplane, ship and school bus.

Thinking About Thinking
    Teacher Comment: **What did you think about to decide what kind of vehicle is shown the picture?**
      Student Response:
      1. I looked at each picture and saw where the vehicle moves.
      2. I looked for the word for that kind of vehicle.

Personal Application
    Teacher Comment: **Why is it important to know whether vehicles travel on land, sea, or in the air.**
      Student Response: I need to know where vehicles travel to tell or write about them.

Kindergarten Thinking Skills & Key Concepts — Teacher's Manual

Pages 127 - KINDS OF VEHICLES

TEACHING SUGGESTION
- Young children may not know the meaning of "emergency." Explain that an emergency is an event such as an accident, injury, illness, or crime that threatens the life or safety of a person. Ask students to identify some workers who help people in an emergency.
- Define the following classes: emergency vehicles, public transportation, and recreation vehicles.
- Clarify why and how emergency vehicles must move quickly.
- Explain that "public" means "everyone," so public transportation means that anyone may ride on that vehicle from one place to another.
- Recreation is an activity that people enjoy.

Introduction
Teacher Comment: **People use some vehicles that carry many people to work or to school each day. Those vehicles are called "transportation vehicles." Some vehicles get help quickly for people in danger. Those vehicles are called "emergency vehicles." Some vehicles are used for fun. Those vehicles are called "recreation vehicles."**

Explaining the Objective to Students
Teacher Comment: **In this lesson you will identify types of vehicles by naming how they are used.**

Conducting the Lesson
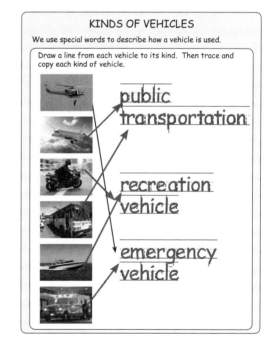

Teacher Comment: **Name the first vehicle.**
  Student Response: That vehicle is a helicopter.
Teacher Comment: **What is a helicopter used for?**
  Student Response: A helicopter is sometimes used to rescue people at sea or to get accident victims to help quickly by flying over traffic.
Teacher Comment: **What kind of vehicle is a helicopter?**
  Student Response: A helicopter is an emergency vehicle.
Teacher Comment: **A line is drawn from the picture of the helicopter to the words "emergency vehicle."**
Teacher Comment: **Trace and copy the words "emergency vehicle."**
Teacher Comment: **Name the second vehicle.**
  Student Response: That vehicle is an airplane
Teacher Comment: **What is an airplane used for?**
  Student Response: An airplane moves people long distances. Anyone may buy a ticket to travel from one city to another.
Teacher Comment: **What kind of vehicle is an airplane?**
  Student Response: An airplane is a public transportation vehicle.
Teacher Comment: **Draw a line from the picture of the airplane to the words "public transportation."**
Teacher Comment: **Trace and copy the words "public transportation."**

Teacher Comment: **Name the third vehicle.**
  Student Response: That vehicle is a motorcycle.
Teacher Comment: **What is a motorcycle used for?**
  Student Response: Most motorcycle owners use their motorcycles for fun. Some people use their motorcycles to go to work, but most drivers use a motorcycle because they enjoy the ride and can go in places that they can not reach in cars.
Teacher Comment: **What kind of vehicle is a motorcycle?**
  Student Response: A motorcycle is a recreation vehicle.
Teacher Comment: **Draw a line from the picture of the motorcycle to the words "recreation vehicle." Trace and copy the words "recreation vehicle."**

Teacher Comment: **Name the next vehicle.**
   Student Response: That vehicle is a bus.
Teacher Comment: **What is a bus used for?**
   Student Response: A bus carries people around the city. Anyone can pay a fare to get on and off the bus at different stops.
Teacher Comment: **What kind of vehicle is a bus?**
   Student Response: A bus is "public transportation."
Teacher Comment: **Draw a line from the picture of the bus to the words "public transportation."**

Teacher Comment: **Name the next vehicle.**
   Student Response: That vehicle is a motorboat.
Teacher Comment: **What is a motorboat used for?**
   Student Response: A motorboat is used for enjoyment. People like the speed of driving a fast boat over lakes, rivers, or the ocean.
Teacher Comment: **What kind of vehicle is a motorboat?**
   Student Response: A motorboat belongs to the class "recreation vehicle."
Teacher Comment: **Draw a line from the picture of the motorboat to the words "recreation vehicle."**

Teacher Comment: **Name the last vehicle.**
   Student Response: That vehicle is an ambulance.
Teacher Comment: **What is an ambulance used for?**
   Student Response: An ambulance goes quickly to a person who is very sick or injured and carries that person to a hospital.
Teacher Comment: **What kind of vehicle is an ambulance?**
   Student Response: An ambulance is an emergency vehicle.
Teacher Comment: **Draw a line from the picture of the ambulance to the words "emergency vehicle."**

Thinking About Thinking
   Teacher Comment: **What did you think about to decide what kind of vehicle is shown the picture?**
   Student Response:
   1. I looked at each picture and named the vehicle.
   2. I remembered how it is used.
   3. I looked for the word for that kind of vehicle.

Personal Application
   Teacher Comment: **When is it important to describe a kind of vehicle?**
   Student Response: I name the kind of vehicle to describe it correctly and to write about it.

Page 128 - KINDS OF VEHICLES

LESSON

- As students explain which vehicle is not like the others, they are identifying the exception. Encourage students to use words that show how the vehicle is different: but, not, different, instead of, and unlike.

Introduction
Teacher Comment: **In the last lesson we named kinds of vehicle: emergency vehicles, public transportation vehicles, and recreation vehicles.**

Explaining the Objective to Students
Teacher Comment: **In this lesson you will identify a vehicle that is not the same kind as the others.**

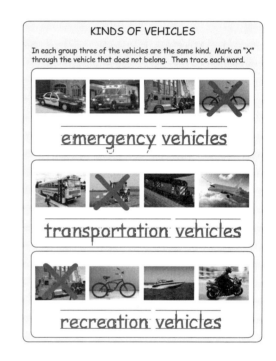

Conducting the Lesson
Teacher Comment: **Name the emergency vehicles in the first row.**
Student Response: The police car, the ambulance, and the fire truck are emergency vehicles.
Teacher Comment: **Which vehicle is not an emergency vehicle?**
Student Response: The bicycle is not an emergency vehicle.
Teacher Comment: **Mark an "X" over the bicycle picture. Trace the words "emergency vehicles."**

- Continue this dialog for transportation vehicles and recreation vehicles.

Thinking About Thinking
Teacher Comment: **What did you think about to decide which vehicle is not the same kind as the others?**
Student Response
1. I looked at pictures of various vehicles and looked for the word that describes three of those vehicles.
2. I identified the vehicle that does not fit that group and explained why.

Personal Application
Teacher Comment: **When is it important to explain which vehicle is different from others?**
Student Response: I need to describe deliveries, describe traffic, or to give directions when using public transportation.

Kindergarten Thinking Skills & Key Concepts   Teacher's Manual

Page 129 - KINDS OF VEHICLES

LESSON

Introduction
   Teacher Comment: **In the last lesson we decided which vehicle did not belong to a group.**

Stating the Objective
   Teacher Comment: **In this lesson you will complete a sentence to describe a vehicle.**

Conducting the Lesson
   Teacher Comment: **Name the vehicle in the top box.**
      Student Response: That vehicle is a school bus.
   Teacher Comment: **A school bus carries many passengers. It is a transportation vehicle. Trace the sentence, "A school bus is a transportation vehicle."**

   Teacher Comment: **Name the vehicle in the second box.**
      Student Response: That vehicle is an ambulance.
   Teacher Comment: **An ambulance is an emergency vehicle that takes injured or sick people to the hospital. Use words in the WORD BOX to write a sentence to describe an ambulance.**
      Student Response: An ambulance is an emergency vehicle.
   Teacher Comment: **Write that sentence on the blanks.**

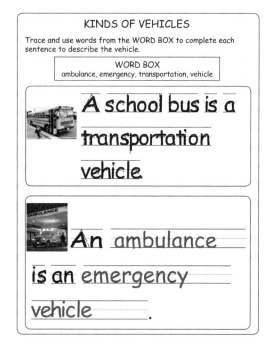

Thinking About Thinking
   Teacher Comment: **What did you think about to describe the kind of vehicle shown in the picture?**
      Student Response:
      1. I looked at each picture and identified the vehicle.
      2. I remembered the important details about that vehicle (size, how it is used, how many people it can carry, where it is driven).
      3. I looked for the words that describe that kind of vehicle.
      4. I finished a sentence that names the vehicle and tells what kind of vehicle it is.

Personal Application
   Teacher Comment: **When is it important to describe a kind of vehicle?**
      Student Response: I name the kind of vehicle to describe it correctly and write about it.

Kindergarten Thinking Skills & Key Concepts — Teacher's Manual

Page 130 - MATCH DRIVERS TO THEIR VEHICLES

LESSON

Introduction
Teacher Comment: We have studied occupations and different kinds of vehicles.

Stating the Objective
Teacher Comment: In this lesson you will match a worker to the vehicle that the worker drives.

Conducting the Lesson
Teacher Comment: **A construction worker usually drives a pickup truck to carry tools, equipment, and building materials. A line has been drawn from the picture of a construction worker to the picture of a pickup truck.**

Teacher Comment: **What vehicle does a firefighter drive?**
  Student Response: A firefighter drives a fire truck.
Teacher Comment: **Draw a line from firefighter to fire truck.**

Teacher Comment: **What vehicle does a boy drive?**
  Student Response: A boy often rides a bicycle.
Teacher Comment: **Draw a line from boy to bicycle.**

Teacher Comment: **What vehicle does a pilot drive?**
  Student Response: A pilot flies an airplane.
Teacher Comment: **Draw a line from pilot to airplane.**

Teacher Comment: **What vehicle does a police officer drive?**
  Student Response: A police officer drives a police car.
Teacher Comment: **Draw a line from police officer to police car.**

Thinking About Thinking
Teacher Comment: **What did you think about in order to match a person's job to the vehicle used in that occupation?**
  Student Response:
  1. I looked at the details of the driver in the picture.
  2. I named that driver.
  3. I found the vehicle that he drives.
  4. I drew a line from the driver to the vehicle.

Personal Application
Teacher Comment: **When do you describe the vehicle that is driven by a person in his or her work?**
  Student Response: I describe the vehicle that a person drives to tell about their work and the training that they may need to drive the vehicle.

CHAPTER ELEVEN – THINKING ABOUT BUILDINGS (Pages 132-142)

TEACHING ABOUT BUILDINGS

CURRICULUM APPLICATIONS
Social Studies: Identify how a family or community depends upon the products and services produced or located in buildings. Identify examples of types of buildings, (residences, government buildings, recreational buildings, storage buildings, and stores) and identify their key characteristics (structure, appearance, ownership, and people who use it)

LANGUAGE INTEGRATION ACTIVITIES
- A list of buildings described in this chapter is provided in the appendix. To help students associate the word with the picture of the building, enlarge this list for display and refer to the term for various buildings as you teach the lesson.
- Drawing: Ask students to draw a picture of an apartment building, a post office, or a library. Students may write or give short descriptions of the building.
- Select a common story or fairy tale about a building, such as *The Little House* by Virginia Lee Burton. Ask students to retell the story about another building (for example substituting an apartment for a house). Discuss how the revised story is different from the original. For instance, although the little house could be moved, an apartment building is too large to move. It might be renovated or used for another purpose.
- Listening: Prior to a lesson that features a building, read aloud a non-fiction picture book about that building. Language experiences with books extend this lesson. After discussing any picture book ask the following questions:
  Are there any new ideas about (apartment buildings, post offices, libraries, etc.) that we learned from this story?
  What ideas or details about (apartment buildings, post offices, libraries, etc.) did you learn from the pictures?
  Is this information true of most (apartment buildings, post offices, libraries, etc.)?

TEACHING SUGGESTIONS
- Encourage students to give examples from their local community of the locations where the buildings described in this lesson are located.
- "Dwellings" or "residences" are abstract concepts for most young children. Dwellings can refer to homes for animals, as well as people; residences refers only to people. Use the terms "dwellings" or "residences" often in these activities and in other contexts and encourage students to do so.
- Teachers may use the following graphic organizer for bulletin board displays, student art work, or end-of-unit summary lessons. For a blank graph, see the appendix.

MENTAL MODEL

A mental model is a framework for understanding a concept. It outlines the characteristics that one must state to describe or define a concept. After completing this chapter, each kindergarten student will have applied this mental model to vehicles in the lessons. A mental model helps a student:

- Anticipate what he or she needs to know to understand a new building
- Remember the characteristics of a building
- State a clear definition or write an adequate description of a building
- Explain a building to someone else

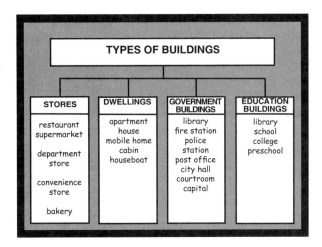

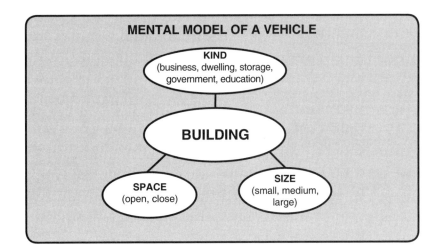

Page 132 - DESCRIBING BUILDINGS
LESSON

Introduction
Select a familiar building and describe it to the class in three to five sentences.
  Teacher Comment: **Name the building I described.**
  Teacher Comment: **What clues let you know what building I described?**
  Student Response: Students cite size, location, what it is used for, etc.

Stating the Objective
  Teacher Comment: **In this lesson I will describe a building and you will select it.**

Conducting the Lesson
  Teacher Comment: **This building can be moved on wheels so that it can be pulled by a car or truck. Some can be as big as a small house. Some people use this building as their permanent home. Other people live in one while traveling or on vacation. What do we call this building?**
  Student Response: This building is a mobile home.
  Teacher Comment: **Circle the picture of the mobile home.**

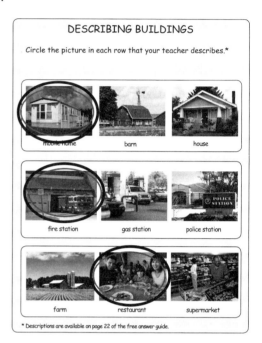

  Teacher Comment: **What clues let you know that the building is the mobile home?**
  Student Response: It can be moved. It is a small home that some people live in all the time.
  Teacher Comment: **Why don't the other buildings fit the description?**
  Student Response: A barn is not a home for people. Neither a barn nor a house is movable.

  Teacher Comment: **Look at the second row. Firefighters and their equipment are located in a large building. It has a large open area that looks like a garage and is used to store the fire truck. Firefighters usually spend the night in this building while they are on duty. Firefighters spend time there getting their equipment ready, exercising, and practicing rescue skills. What do we call this building?**
  Student Response: This building is a fire station.
  Teacher Comment: **Circle the picture of the fire station.**

  Teacher Comment: **What clues let you know that the building is the fire station?**
  Student Response: It is a large building with large doors so that fire trucks can be stored and worked on inside.
  Teacher Comment: **Why don't the other buildings fit the description?**
  Student Response: A gas station is a business that sells fuel, not an emergency service building. A police station does not have such large doors for a storage area for large vehicles.

  Teacher Comment: **Look at the last row. This business is a place where people sometimes go to eat. Customers sit at a table or a counter. A server asks what customers want to eat, gets food from the cooks, and brings it to the customer. The customer must pay for the food before leaving. What do we call this building?**
  Student Response: This building is a restaurant.
  Teacher Comment: **Circle the picture of the restaurant.**

  Teacher Comment: **What clues let you know that the building is the restaurant?**
  Student Response: Many customers are seated at many tables, eating or waiting for their food. Servers bring food to customers who are seated at tables.
  Teacher Comment: **Why don't the other buildings fit the description?**
  Student Response: A farm and supermarket also sell food, but in those buildings people do not sit down and eat food that a cook prepares.

Thinking About Thinking
  Teacher Comment: **What did you look for when you picked the building that was described?**
  Student Response:
  1. I recalled the important details of the building (its size, what it is used for, who owns it, and what kind of building it is).
  2. I found the important details in the pictures.
  3. I checked that the pictures of other buildings do not show those important details.

Personal Application
  Teacher Comment: **When is it important to describe buildings well?**
  Student Response: It is important to describe buildings in order to describe trips; to give directions; to find places.

Page 133 - DESCRIBING BUILDINGS

LESSON

Introduction
  Teacher Comment: **We have selected a building from its description.**

Stating the Objective
  Teacher Comment: **In this lesson you will describe a building.**

Conducting the Lesson
  Teacher Comment: **Name the first building and describe it to your partner.**

  Student Response: A library is a large building with rows of shelves. People go there to read or borrow books, magazines, CD's, videotapes, and audiotapes. People read books and magazines and use computers there. Libraries are usually owned by the government of the town or county. Anyone can get a free or inexpensive card to check out material.
  Teacher Comment: **Trace and copy the word "library" on the lines.**

  Teacher Comment: **What details do you describe to explain that building in the photograph is a library?**
  Student Response: I described its size, what people do there, and how books and other material are stored there.

  Teacher Comment: **Look at the second building. Name this building and describe it to your partner.**
  Student Response: A post office is a place where people send letters and packages. In large cities, the post office workers sort the mail and send it to other post offices. In small towns, a post office may look like a small store or may be a section of the store. The post office is owned by our national government. People buy stamps there to pay for delivering the mail.
  Teacher Comment: **Trace and copy the words "post office."**
  Teacher Comment: **What details do you describe to explain that the building in the photograph is a post office?**
  Student Response: I described what people do there, the service it provides, and that it is a government building.

Teacher Comment: **Look at the bottom building. Name this building and describe it to your partner.**
  Student Response: An apartment is a small residence inside a large apartment building. It is a group of rooms with a living room, bedrooms, bathrooms, and a kitchen used by one family. Because it has many families living in it, an apartment building is bigger than a house. Halls or stairs may be used by all the families in the apartment building. Large cities have many apartment buildings to house many families in one building.
Teacher Comment: **Trace and copy the word "apartment."**
Teacher Comment: **What details do you describe to explain that the building in the photograph is an apartment building?**
  Student Response: I described the small residences inside a large apartment building. The apartments look alike from the outside because there are many of them on many floors.

Thinking About Thinking
Teacher Comment: **What did you say to describe a building?**
  Student Response:
  1. I recalled the important details of the building (what one looks like, its purpose, who lives or works there, how it is constructed, etc.).
  2. I checked that I described all those important details.
  3. I checked that I have given enough details to keep the building I am describing from being confused for other kinds of buildings.

Personal Application
Teacher Comment: **When is it important to describe buildings well?**
  Student Response: It is important to describe buildings in order to describe trips, to give directions, or to find places

PAGE 134 - DESCRIBING BUILDINGS

LESSON

Introduction
Teacher Comment: **In the last lesson we described buildings.**

Stating the Objective
Teacher Comment: **In this lesson you will match a photograph of a building to its name.**

Conducting the Lesson
Teacher Comment: **Name the building shown in the first photograph.**
  Student Response: That building is a fire station.
Teacher Comment: **Notice that a line is drawn from the photograph of the fire station to its name. Trace and copy the words "fire station."**
Teacher Comment: **What details in the photograph show that it is a fire station?**
  Student Response: The fire station has a fire engine parked in front of it.

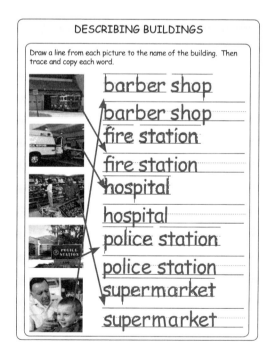

Teacher Comment: **Name the building in the second photograph.**
  Student Response: That building is a hospital.
Teacher Comment: **What details in the photograph show that it is a hospital?**
  Student Response: The ambulance is parked at the door. Emergency workers roll a sick or injured person inside
Teacher Comment: **Find "hospital" in the list of words and draw a line from the photograph to the word "hospital." Trace and copy the word "hospital."**

- Continue this dialog for supermarket, police station, and barber shop.

Thinking About Thinking
  Teacher Comment: **How did you decide which word belonged with each photograph?**
  Student Response:
  1. I looked at the details
  2. I named the building.
  3. I looked for its name.

Personal Application
  Teacher Comment: **When is it important to match building names?**
  Student Response: It is important to describe buildings correctly to read and write about them.

Page 135 - DESCRIBING BUILDINGS - SIZE

Introduction
  Teacher Comment: **We describe a building as small, medium, or large compared to other buildings.**

Stating the Objective
  Teacher Comment: **In this lesson you will describe buildings by their size.**

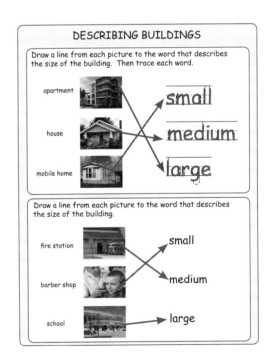

Conducting the Lesson
  Teacher Comment: **Name the buildings in the first box.**
    Student Response: The buildings are an apartment, a house, and a mobile home.
  Teacher Comment: **The pictures make the buildings look like they are the same size. Look at the surroundings and what you know about the buildings to decide its size.**
  Teacher Comment: **Which building is small?**
    Student Response: The mobile home is small.
  Teacher Comment: **Draw a line from the mobile home to the word "small" and trace the word "small."**

  Teacher Comment: **Which building is the largest?**
    Student Response: The apartment building is the largest.
  Teacher Comment: **Draw a line from the apartment to the word "large" and trace the word "large."**

  Teacher Comment: **Which building is medium in size?**
    Student Response: The house is medium in size.
  Teacher Comment: **Draw a line from the house to the word "medium" and trace the word "medium.**

  Teacher Comment: **In the bottom box draw a line from each picture to the word that describes the size of the building.**

Thinking About Thinking
Teacher Comment: **What did you think about to describe the size of buildings.**
Student Response:
1. I remembered the size of the building and what I saw in the picture.
2. I thought about how big it is compared to other buildings.
3. I described it as small, medium, or large.

Personal Application
Teacher Comment: **When is it important to describe the size of a building?**
Student Response: I need to describe the size of a building when I write a story about it or compare it to others.

Page 136 - DESCRIBING PARTS OF A HOUSE

LESSON

Introduction
Teacher Comment: **To describe a building, we need to know the names of its parts and explain how each part is important for the building to last a long time and to meet the needs of the people who use it.**

Stating the Objective
Teacher Comment: **In this lesson you will think about the parts of a house, what each part does, and what would happen to the house if that part was missing or damaged.**

Conducting the Lesson
Teacher Comment: **Name the top part of the house.**
Student Response: The top part of the house is the roof.
Teacher Comment: **Write the word "roof" in the top box.**
Teacher Comment: **How does the roof keep the house strong and safe?**
Student Response: The roof covers the house, keeps out rain, and keeps the rooms comfortable. The roof helps to hold the walls together.
Teacher Comment: **What would happen if the roof was missing or damaged?**
Student Response: Rain or snow would damage the inside of the house. The people in the house would be cold in winter and hot in summer. The walls of the house would become weak.

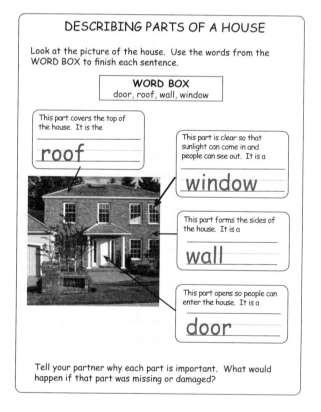

Teacher Comment: **Name the clear part of the sides.**
Student Response: The clear part of the house is a window.
Teacher Comment: **Write the word "window" on the blank lines in the second box.**

Teacher Comment: **Why must a house have windows?**
Student Response: The windows let in light and air and allow people who live in the house to see outside.
Teacher Comment: **What would happen if the windows were missing or damaged?**
Student Response: If the house had no windows, the rooms would be dark and people could not see out. If the glass in the window was missing or damaged, rain would damage the rooms inside and the people who live in the house would be uncomfortable.

Teacher Comment: **Name the sides of the house.**
Student Response: The side of a house is a wall. Walls hold the house together.
Teacher Comment: **Write the word "wall" in the third box.**

Teacher Comment: **Why must a house have walls?**
Student Response: The walls hold up the roof for shelter and keep out the weather. The walls keep the people who live in the house safe and comfortable.
Teacher Comment: **What would happen if a wall was missing or damaged?**
Student Response: If a wall was missing or damaged, rain or snow would get into the house and damage the insides. The people who live in the house would not feel safe and comfortable.

Teacher Comment: **What part is the entrance to the house.**
Student Response: The door is the entrance to the house.
Teacher Comment: **Why must a house have a door?**
Student Response: The door keeps the people and things inside safe. The door keeps the rain or snow out and helps the people inside stay comfortable.
Teacher Comment: **Write the word "door" in the bottom box.**
Teacher Comment: **What would happen if the door were missing or damaged?**
Student Response: Weather or other people could get into the house.

Thinking About Thinking
Teacher Comment: **What did you think about in order to describe the parts of a house?**
Student Response:
1. I named the part.
2. I remembered what it is used for.
3. I thought about what would happen if that part was missing.

Personal Application
Teacher Comment: **When is it important to describe parts of a building?**
Student Response: I describe the parts of a building to tell or write a story about it.

PAGE 137 - SIMILAR BUILDINGS

TEACHING SUGGESTIONS
- Emphasize the wording commonly used to describe similarities. Repeat words that show similarity (both, and, like, similar, resemble, also, etc.) and encourage students to use them in their responses.
- Some teachers reinforce students' responses by writing their comments on the HOW ARE TWO THINGS ALIKE diagram shown in the appendix. See the example at the right. Use a transparency or draw the diagram on chart paper or display board. Students begin to associate their answers with the words that they see on the diagram. However, if writing on the diagram distracts young children from thinking about the topic, using this method may not be helpful.

LESSON

Introduction
Teacher Comment: **In the last lesson we described the parts of a house.**

Stating the Objective
Teacher Comment: **In this lesson you will identify a building that is most like another building.**

Conducting the Lesson
Teacher Comment: **Look at the example at the top of the page. The building on the left is a house. Name the buildings shown on the right.**

Student Response: The buildings are a school, an apartment building, and a barn.

Teacher Comment: **Tell your partner all the important things that you know about a house.**

Student Response: A house is a building where one or two families live. Families sleep, prepare their food, store their belongings, and stay safe and warm in houses.

Teacher Comment: **Which building at the right is most like a house?**

Student Response: An apartment building is most like a house.

Teacher Comment: **How is an apartment most like a house?**

Student Response: Both are places where families sleep, prepare their food, store their belongings, and stay safe and warm.

Teacher Comment: **How are the other buildings different from a house?**

Student Response: A school is a place where children learn. They do not live there. A farm is a place where people raise animals and plants, but a farm is not necessarily the home of the farmer.

Teacher Comment: **Notice a circle is drawn around the photograph of the apartment building to show that it is like a house.**

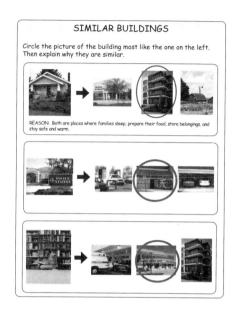

Teacher Comment: **Look at the second row. The building on the left is a police station. Name the buildings shown on the right.**

Student Response: The buildings are a gas station, a fire station, and a garage.

Teacher Comment: **Tell your partner all the important things that you know about a police station.**

Student Response: A police station is the place where police officers meet and keep their equipment.

Teacher Comment: **Which building at the right is most like a police station?**

Student Response: A fire station is most like a police station.

Teacher Comment: **How is a fire station most like a police station?**

Student Response: Both are a place where emergency workers keep their equipment and stay until they are called to help people. Both are buildings that are owned by the city or county government.

Teacher Comment: **How are the other buildings different from a police station?**

Student Response: A gas station is a store where people go to buy gasoline. It is a business, not a government building. A garage is a building used to store vehicles, not a government building.

Teacher Comment: **Circle the fire station.**

Teacher Comment: **Look at the third row. The building on the left is a library. Name the buildings on the right.**

Student Response: The buildings on the right are a hospital, a school, and an apartment building.

Teacher Comment: **Tell your partner all the important things that you know about a library.**

Student Response: A library is a building where people get free information. They may read or borrow books, magazines, or movies. Libraries are usually operated by the government.

Teacher Comment: **Which building at the right is most like a library?**

Student Response: A school is most like a library.

Teacher Comment: **How is a school most like a library?**

Student Response: Both are buildings where people go to get information. Both buildings have books and computers. Children visit both buildings. Most libraries and schools are operated by the government.
Teacher Comment: **How are the other buildings different from a library?**
Student Response: An apartment building is a place where many families live. A hospital treats injured and ill people.
Teacher Comment: **Circle the school.**

Thinking About Thinking
Teacher Comment: **What did you say to describe similar buildings?**
Student Response:
1. I recalled the important details of the first building (its appearance, special equipment, etc.).
2. I looked for similar details in the other buildings.
3. I selected the building that has most of the same details.
4. I checked to see that other buildings do not fit the important details better than the one I selected.

Personal Application
Teacher Comment: **When is it important to understand how building are alike?**
Student Response: I need to understand how buildings are alike to recognize buildings that are similar to ones I already know, or to describe a building to someone who is unfamiliar with it.

Page 138 - SIMILAR BUILDINGS

TEACHING SUGGESTIONS
- Emphasize the wording commonly used to describe similarities. Repeat words that show similarity (both, and, like, similar, resemble, also, etc.) and encourage students to use them in their responses.
- "Dwellings" or "residences" are abstract concepts for most young children. Since they have heard these terms several times in previous exercises, students should begin to use them independently, if they have frequent practice doing so. Dwellings can refer to homes for animals, as well as people; residences refers only to people. Use the terms "dwellings" or "residences" often in these activities and in other contexts and encourage students to do so. Acknowledge students' unprompted use of these terms..
- Some Teachers reinforce students' responses by writing their comments on the HOW ARE TWO THINGS ALIKE diagram shown in the appendix. See the example at the right. Use a transparency or draw the diagram on chart paper or display board. Students begin to associate their answers with the words that they see on the diagram. However, if writing on the diagram distracts young children from thinking about the topic, using this method may not be helpful.

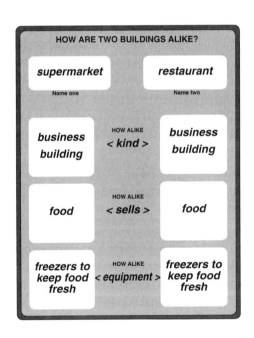

LESSON

Introduction
Teacher Comment: **In the last lesson we found a building that was most like another building.**

Stating the Objective
Teacher Comment: **In this lesson you will explain how two buildings are alike.**

Conducting the Lesson
Teacher Comment: **Look at the first pair of buildings, read the names of the buildings shown in the photographs.**
Student Response: The buildings are a restaurant and a supermarket.

Teacher Comment: **How are these buildings alike?**
Student Response: Both are places people go to get food. People who work there help customers buy the food they want. Customers must pay before taking food out. People can buy prepared food in both stores. Both contain refrigerators, freezers, and clean shelves to keep food fresh and safe to eat.
Teacher Comment: **Trace the words "restaurant" and "supermarket."**

Teacher Comment: **Look at the second pair of buildings and read their names.**
Teacher Comment: **How are these places alike?**
Student Response: Both are places where children learn and play.
Teacher Comment: **Trace the words "school" and "playground."**

Teacher Comment: **Look at the third pair of buildings and read their names.**
Teacher Comment: **How are these buildings alike?**
Student Response: Both buildings have large doors for vehicles. Both may be heated or unheated. Tools are stored there.
Teacher Comment: **Trace the words "barn" and "garage."**

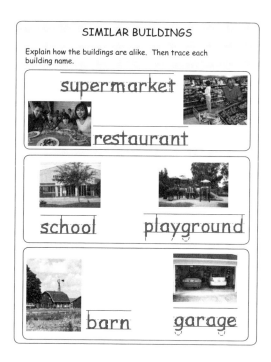

Thinking About Thinking
Teacher Comment: **What did you explain about buildings to tell how they are alike?**
Student Response:
1. I explained its size, what it is used for, who lives or works there, who owns it, its appearance.
2. I explained details that both buildings have.
3. I checked that I explained the important details of both buildings.

Personal Application
Teacher Comment: **When is it important to understand how buildings are alike?**
Student Response: It's important to understand how buildings are alike to give or understand directions. I need to understand why their construction, location, or use may be similar when I explain a particular building to someone.

PAGE 139 - SIMILARITIES AND DIFFERENCES

TEACHING SUGGESTIONS
- Explain the term "unlike" and encourage students to use words that cue differences (but, not, different, opposite, and unlike).
- To help young children express contrast, emphasize the use of the conjunction "but." Example: A house stays in one place, but a mobile home may be moved. Explain that "but" is a signal word to alert the reader or listener that what comes after it will be different than what came before it. Encourage students to use this sentence pattern and acknowledge students' unprompted statements expressing contrast using this syntax.
- When contrasting buildings, students sometimes answer with a detail about only one of the buildings. For example, if the student answers that a mobile home can be moved. Confirm that it is correct that a mobile home is built so it can be moved. Then ask whether the house is built so it can be moved. The student then realizes that the house is built to stay where it is. The student has now contrasted whether or not the building is built to be moved.

LESSON

Introduction
Teacher Comment: **When we described how buildings are alike, we compared them. Sometimes we want to know how they are different in order to understand something important about them. When we describe how buildings are different, we contrast them.**

Stating the Objective
Teacher Comment: **In this lesson you will explain how two buildings are alike <u>and</u> how they are different.**

Conducting the Lesson
Teacher Comment: **Look at the first pair of buildings. You see a mobile home and a house. Trace the words "mobile home" and "house." How are these buildings alike?**

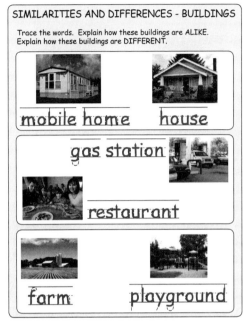

Student Response: Both are buildings people live or work in; they come in different sizes; a family can live in them.

Teacher Comment: **How are these buildings different?**
Student Response: A house is designed to stay in one place, but a mobile home can be moved to a different location at any time. Houses are made of wood or concrete and sit on a concrete foundation, but a mobile home is made of aluminum or metal and sits on a steel frame. Some mobile homes have wheels and can be pulled by a car or truck. A house is too large to move along the highway and is built on a foundation, not wheels.

Teacher Comment: **Look at the second pair of buildings. You see a gas station and a restaurant. Trace the words "restaurant" and "gas station."**
Teacher Comment: **How are these buildings alike?**
Student Response: Both are places where people go to buy something they need; someone owns the business. People work there. People do not live in these places, they are used for business.

Teacher Comment: **How are these buildings different?**
Student Response: A gas station provides gasoline for a vehicle, but a restaurant provides a place for people to eat. At some gas stations you can buy snacks to eat, but at a restaurant you cannot buy gasoline. In restaurants many people can sit inside and eat. Gas stations serve several cars at one time outside.

Teacher Comment: **Look at the third pair of buildings. You see a farm and a playground. Trace the words "farm" and "playground." How are these buildings alike?**
Student Response: Both are usually in large open spaces. Equipment that people use to work or play can be found on them. While some farmers live on their farms, both are usually not residences.

Teacher Comment: **How are these buildings different?**
Student Response: People can live on a farm, but not on a playground. A farm is a place where food is grown and animals are raised; people work there. A playground is a place people go to have fun, it is used for recreation, mostly by children. The equipment on a farm is used to do a job, but playground equipment is used as rides or enjoyment. The animals that live on a farm belong to the farmer and are usually raised for food and sold at some time.

Thinking About Thinking
Teacher Comment: **What did you explain about buildings to tell how they are alike or different?**
Student Response:
1. I explained their size, what it is used for, who lives or works there, and who owns it.
2. I explained similar details of the two buildings.
3. I explained the different details in the two buildings.
4. I checked to see that I have explained the important details of both buildings.

Personal Application
Teacher Comment: **When is it important to tell how buildings are alike and how they are different?**
Student Response: It's important to tell how buildings are alike and how they are different to give or understand directions; to understand why the construction, location, or use of buildings may be similar; to explain a particular building to someone who is unfamiliar with it.

Kindergarten Thinking Skills & Key Concepts   Teacher's Manual

Page 140 - KINDS OF BUILDINGS

Introduction
  Teacher Comment: **In this lesson you will learn about different kinds of buildings. Some buildings are businesses where we buy the things or services that we want. Some buildings are owned by the government and provide services we need. Buildings where people live are called residences. Some buildings are used to store things.**

Stating the Objective
  Teacher Comment: **In this lesson you will match a photograph of a building to the group in which it belongs.**

Conducting the Lesson
  Teacher Comment: **Name the building shown in the first photograph.**
    Student Response: The first building is a post office.
  Teacher Comment: **What details in the photograph show that it is a post office?**
    Student Response: The name on the building and the red, white, and blue sign show that the building is a post office.
  Teacher Comment: **What kind of building is a post office?**
    Student Response: A post office is a government building.
  Teacher Comment: **Notice that a line is drawn from the photograph of the post office to the word that describes its kind. Trace and copy the word "government."**

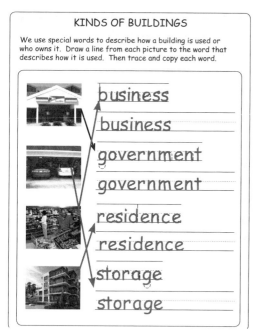

  Teacher Comment: **Name the building shown in the second photograph.**
    Student Response: That building is a garage.
  Teacher Comment: **What details in the photograph show that it is a garage?**
    Student Response: The two cars inside the building show that it is a garage. The cars go into the garage through the very large door that slides up to let them in. Tools and other things are stored along the wall of the garage.
  Teacher Comment: **What kind of building is a garage?**
    Student Response: A garage is a storage building
  Teacher Comment: **Draw a line from the photograph to the word "storage." Copy and trace the word "storage."**

  Teacher Comment: **Name the building shown in the third photograph.**
    Student Response: That building is a supermarket
  Teacher Comment: **What details in the photograph show that it is a supermarket?**
    Student Response: This large building has rows of shelves that hold food. Customers push carts to hold the food they need.
  Teacher Comment: **What kind of building is a supermarket?**
    Student Response: A supermarket is a business.
  Teacher Comment: **Draw a line from the photograph to the word "business." Trace and copy the word "business."**

  Teacher Comment: **Name the building shown in the last photograph.**
    Student Response: That building is an apartment building.
  Teacher Comment: **What details in the photograph show that it is an apartment building?**
    Student Response: This large building has many apartments on many floors.
  Teacher Comment: **What kind of building is an apartment building?**
    Student Response: An apartment building is a residence.
  Teacher Comment: **Draw a line from the photograph to the word "residence." Trace and copy the word "residence."**

Thinking About Thinking
 Teacher Comment: **What did you think about to decide what kind of building is shown the picture?**
 Student Response:
 1. I looked at each picture and named the building.
 2. I remembered how it is used.
 3. I looked for the word for that kind of building.

Personal Application
 Teacher Comment: **When is it important to describe a kind of building?**
 Student Response: I name the kind of building to describe it correctly and to write about it.

PAGE 141 - KINDS OF BUILDINGS

LESSON
- As students explain which building is not like the others, they are contrasting the buildings and identifying the exception. Encourage students to use words that show how the building is different: but, not, different, instead of, and unlike.

Introduction
 Teacher Comment: **You have written the names of many different kinds of buildings, such as business, emergency, government, health care, residence, and storage.**

Stating the Objective
 Teacher Comment: **In this lesson we will identify a building that is not the same kind as the others.**

Class Activity
 Teacher Comment: **Look at the first row. Name these buildings.**
  Student Response: The buildings are a mobile home, a school, a house, and an apartment.
 Teacher Comment: **How are three of the buildings alike?**
  Student Response: People live in apartment buildings, houses, and mobile homes. Families eat there, sleep there, play there, invite their friends to visit there, and store their belongings there.
 Teacher Comment: **How can we describe this kind of building?**
  Student Response: These buildings are dwellings or residences.
 Teacher Comment: **Notice that the word "residences" is written below the photographs, trace it.**

 Teacher Comment: **Which building is not a residence?**
  Student Response: The school is not a residence. People do not live in a school.
- Note: Young students at residential schools may find this distinction confusing. They should recognize that school is not their permanent home.
 Teacher Comment: **Make an "X" on the photograph of the school.**

 Teacher Comment: **Look at the second set of buildings. Name these four buildings.**
  Student Response: The buildings are a restaurant, a supermarket, a gas station, and a fire station.
 Teacher Comment: **How are three of the buildings alike?**
  Student Response: A restaurant, a supermarket, and a gas station are all businesses where people buy food or gas.
 Teacher Comment: **Notice that the word "businesses" is written below the photographs, trace it.**

Teacher Comment: **Which building doesn't fit that kind?**
　Student Response: A fire station is not a business.
Teacher Comment: **Why is the fire station an exception to this group?**
　Student Response: The fire station is a government building. People do not buy things at a fire station.
Teacher Comment: **Make an "X" on the photograph of the fire station.**

Teacher Comment: **Look at the third set of buildings. Name these four buildings.**
　Student Response: The buildings are a barn, a fire station, a police station, and a post office.
Teacher Comment: **How are three of the buildings alike?**
　Student Response: A fire station, a police station, and a post office are owned by the government.
Teacher Comment: **How can we describe this kind of building?**
　Student Response: These buildings are government buildings.
Teacher Comment: **Notice that the words "government buildings" is written below the photographs, trace it.**

Teacher Comment: **Which building doesn't fit that kind?**
　Student Response: A barn is not a government building.
Teacher Comment: **Why is the barn an exception to this group?**
　Student Response: The barn is a storage building.
Teacher Comment: **Make an "X" on the photograph of the barn.**

Thinking About Thinking
Teacher Comment: **What did you think about to decide which building is not the same as the others?**
　Student Response:
　1. I looked at pictures of various buildings and looked for the word that describes three of those buildings.
　2. I identified the building that does not fit that group and explained why.

Personal Application
Teacher Comment: **When is it important to explain which building is different from others?**
　Student Response: It's important to know how buildings are different to give or understand directions and to tell or to write about a building.

Page 142 – KINDS OF BUILDINGS

LESSON

Introduction
   Teacher Comment: **In the last lesson we have described different kinds of buildings.**

Stating the Objective
   Teacher Comment: **In this lesson you will complete sentences to describe kinds of buildings.**

Conducting the Lesson
   Teacher Comment: **Name the building in the top box.**
     Student Response: That building is a mobile home.
   Teacher Comment: **What kind of building is a mobile home?**
     Student Response: A mobile home is a residence.
   Teacher Comment: **Trace the sentence, "A mobile home is a residence."**

   Teacher Comment: **Name the building in the second box.**
     Student Response: That building is a garage.
   Teacher Comment: **What kind of building is a garage?**
     Student Response: A garage is a storage building.
   Teacher Comment: **Use words in the WORD BOX to complete the sentence to describe the garage.**

   Teacher Comment: **Name the building in the third box.**
     Student Response: That building is a barber shop.
   Teacher Comment: **What kind of building is a barber shop?**
     Student Response: A barber shop is a business.

   Teacher Comment: **Use words in the WORD BOX to complete the sentence to describe the barber shop.**

Thinking About Thinking
   Teacher Comment: **What did you think about to describe the kind of building shown in the picture?**
     Student Response:
     1. I looked at each picture and identified that building.
     2. I remembered the important details about that building (size, purpose, who lives or works there, and equipment it houses).
     3. I looked for the word that describes that kind of building.
     4. I finished a sentence that names the building and tells what kind of building it is.

Personal Application
   Teacher Comment: **When is it important to describe a kind of building?**
     Student Response: I name the kind of building to describe it correctly and write about it.

Kindergarten Thinking Skills & Key Concepts   Teacher's Manual

CHAPTER TWELVE – THINKING AND WRITING ABOUT POSITION
(Pages 144-153)

TEACHING ABOUT POSITION

CURRICULUM APPLICATIONS
Language Arts: Identify and correctly express words that describe location (above/below, inside/outside, front/behind, between, beside); describe location of objects or buildings from written directions or in discussing picture books
Social Studies: Identify location on maps; identify locations of buildings (residences, government buildings, recreational buildings, and stores)
Science: Identify and correctly express the location of parts of organisms, objects, and structures; follow directions in science activities
Art: Identify the location of parts of paintings, sculpture, and other artworks; follow directions in art activities
Physical Education: Follow directions in physical exercises and sports activities

LANGUAGE INTEGRATION ACTIVITIES
- Drawing: Ask students to draw a picture of objects that show given locations or positions. Students may write or tell short stories in which position or location is important.

PICTURE BOOK EXTENSION
- Language experiences with picture books in which location or position is important to the story.

Pages 144-146 - WRITING ABOUT POSITION - ABOVE AND BELOW

LESSON

- Use a sphere and a cube to demonstrate "above" and "below" positions

Introduction
   Teacher Comment: **It is important to be able to describe the position of things.**

Stating the Objective
   Teacher Comment: **In this lesson you will complete sentences that use the words "above" and "below."**

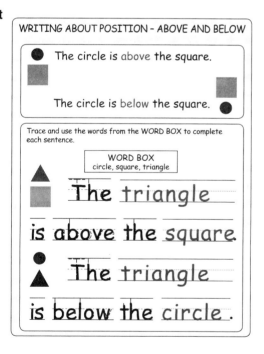

Conducting the Lesson
   Teacher Comment: **Look at the example at the top of the page. Describe the position of the circle in the first drawing.**
      Student Response: The circle is above the square.
   Teacher Comment: **Describe the position of the circle in the second drawing.**
      Student Response: The circle is below the square.
   Teacher Comment: **Now look at the exercise. Which two shapes are shown in the first drawing?**
      Student Response: The shapes are a triangle and a square.
   Teacher Comment: **Which shape is above the other?**
      Student Response: The triangle is above the square.
   Teacher Comment: **Use the WORD BOX to complete the sentence.**

   Teacher Comment: **Which two shapes are shown in the bottom drawing?**
      Student Response: The shapes are a circle and a triangle.
   Teacher Comment: **Which shape is below the other?**
      Student Response: The triangle is below the circle.
   Teacher Comment: **Use the WORD BOX to complete the sentence.**

- Use this dialog to complete the sentences on pages 145-146.

142   © 2015 The Critical Thinking Co.™ • www.CriticalThinking.com • 800-458-4849

Thinking About Thinking

Teacher Comment: **What did you think about in order to write about "above" and "below."**

Student Response:
1. I named the shapes.
2. I decided which shape was above or below the other.
3. I found the word that describes their position.

Personal Application

Teacher Comment: **When is it important to describe position?**

Student Response: I describe position to give directions or tell about the location of people or things in a story.

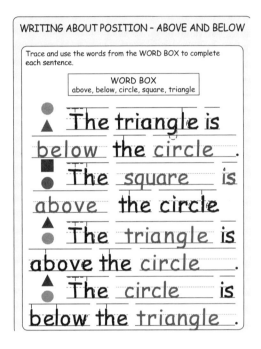

<--------ANSWERS PAGE 145

ANSWERS PAGE 146 ------------------>

Kindergarten Thinking Skills & Key Concepts — Teacher's Manual

Pages 147-148 - WRITING ABOUT POSITION - INSIDE AND OUTSIDE

LESSON

Introduction
  Teacher Comment: **In the last lesson we wrote sentences using the words "above" and "below."**

Stating the Objective
  Teacher Comment: **In this lesson you will complete sentences that use the words "inside" and "outside."**

Conducting the Lesson
  Teacher Comment: **Look at the example at the top of the page. What is the position of the circle?**
    Student Response: The circle is inside the square.
  Teacher Comment: **Describe the second drawing.**
    Student Response: The circle is outside the square.
  Teacher Comment: **Which two shapes are shown in the first exercise?**
    Student Response: The shapes are a circle and a square.
  Teacher Comment: **What is the position of the square?**
    Student Response: The square is inside the circle.
  Teacher Comment: **Use the WORD BOX to complete the sentence**

- Use this dialog to complete the lesson and the lessons on page 148.

Thinking About Thinking
  Teacher Comment: **What did you think about in order to write about "inside" and "outside."**
    Student Response:
    1. I named the shapes.
    2. I decided which shape was inside or outside the other.
    3. I found the words that described their position.

Personal Application
  Teacher Comment: **When is it important to describe position?**
    Student Response: I describe position to give directions or tell about the location of people or things in a story.

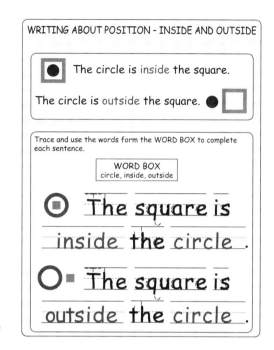

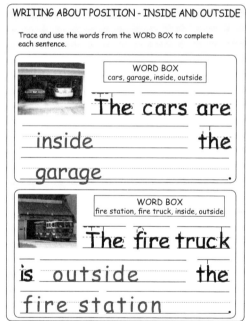

Kindergarten Thinking Skills & Key Concepts — Teacher's Manual

Pages 149-150 - WRITING ABOUT POSITION - FRONT AND BEHIND

LESSON

Introduction
  Teacher Comment: **In the last lesson we wrote sentences using the words "inside" and "outside."**

Stating the Objective
  Teacher Comment: **In this lesson you will complete sentences that use the words "in front of" and "behind."**

Conducting the Lesson
  Teacher Comment: **Describe the objects in the photograph at the top of the page.**
    Student Response: The first photograph shows a ball and a block.
  Teacher Comment: **Which object is behind?**
    Student Response: The block is behind the ball.
  Teacher Comment: **Which object is in front?**
    Student Response: The ball is in front of the block.
  Teacher Comment: **What is the name of solid that looks like a square from all sides?**
    Student Response: A cube looks like a square from all sides
  Teacher Comment: **What do we call the solid that looks like a circle from all sides?**
    Student Response: The sphere looks like a circle from all sides.
  Teacher Comment: **The second photograph shows a red sphere and a cube. Complete the sentences using words from the WORD BOX.**

• Use this dialog to complete the lesson on page 150.

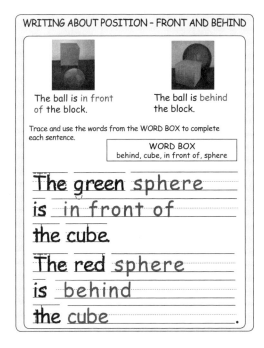

<--------ANSWERS PAGE 149

ANSWERS PAGE 150 ------------------>

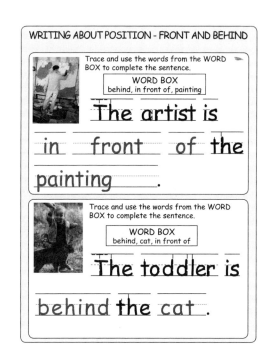

Thinking About Thinking
  Teacher Comment: **What did you think about in order to write about "in front" and "behind."**
    Student Response:
    1. I named the shapes/objects in the picture.
    2. I decided which shape/object was in front or behind the other.
    3. I found the word that describes their position.

Personal Application
  Teacher Comment: **When is it important to describe position?**
    Student Response: I describe position to give directions or tell about the location of people or things in a story.

Kindergarten Thinking Skills & Key Concepts   Teacher's Manual

PAGES 151-153 - WRITING ABOUT POSITION - BETWEEN AND BESIDE

LESSON

Introduction
   Teacher Comment: **In the last lesson we wrote sentences using the words "in front of" and "behind."**

Stating the Objective
   Teacher Comment: **In this lesson you will complete sentences that use the words "between" and "beside."**

Conducting the Lesson
   Teacher Comment: **Look at the example at the top of the page.**
   Teacher Comment: **What is the position of the circle?**
      Student Response: The circle is between the squares.
   Teacher Comment: **Describe the second drawing.**
      Student Response: The circle is beside the square.
   Teacher Comment: **Look at the shapes in the first activity. Describe the position of the square.**
      Student Response: The square is beside the circle.
   Teacher Comment: **Use the WORD BOX and write the words "beside" and "circle" on the blanks.**

- Continue this dialog to discuss the exercises on pages 152-153.

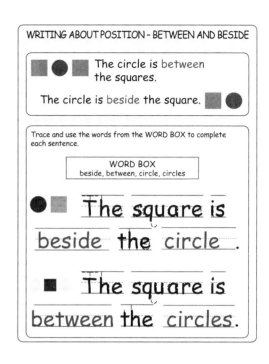

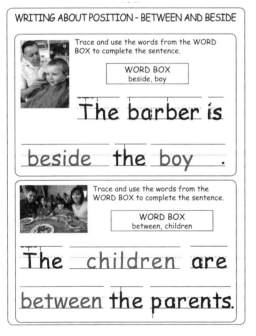

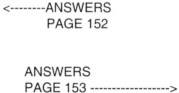
<----------ANSWERS
          PAGE 152

ANSWERS
PAGE 153 ------------------>

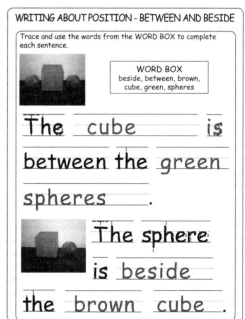

Thinking About Thinking
   Teacher Comment: **What did you think about in order to write about "between" and "beside."**
   Student Response:
   1. I named the shapes.
   2. I decided which shape was between or beside the other.
   3. I found the word that describes their position.

Personal Application
   Teacher Comment: **When is it important to describe position?**
      Student Response: I describe position to give directions or tell about the location of people or things in a story.

APPENDIX
GRAPHIC MASTERS

The following graphics may be used to produce transparencies, bulletin board displays, or to serve as models for diagrams to record students answers on a display board.

1. Cube pattern .... page 148
2. Word list - FOOD .... page 149
3. Word list - ANIMALS .... page 150
4. Word list - JOBS .... page 151
5. Word list - VEHICLES .... page 152
6. Word list - BUILDINGS .... page 153
7. How are two things ALIKE? .... page 154
8. Branching diagram - 2 branches .... page 155
9. Branching diagram - 3 branches .... page 156
10. Branching diagram - 4 branches .... page 157
11. Branching diagram - 5 branches .... page 158

Kindergarten Thinking Skills & Key Concepts Appendix

GRAPHIC MASTER 1 - Cube pattern - use with lesson DESCRIBING SOLIDS - page 39

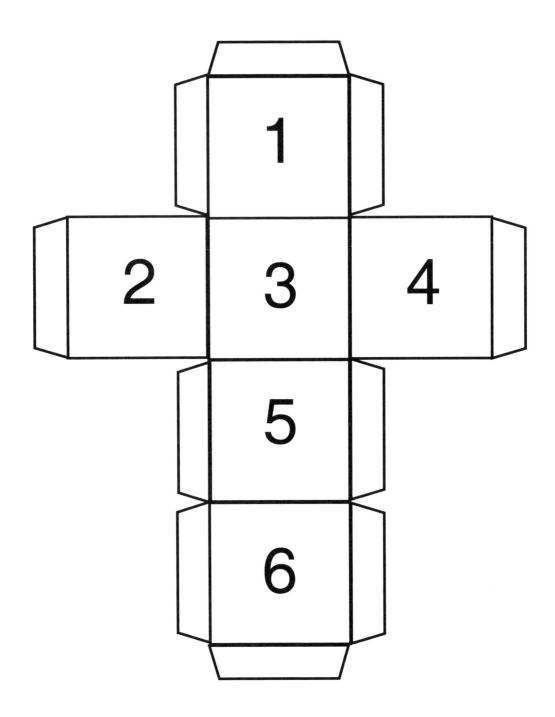

GRAPHIC MASTER 2 - Food list

FOOD

- apple
- bacon
- banana
- beans
- blueberries
- bread
- broccoli
- butter
- cabbage
- carrot
- celery
- cheese
- corn
- eggs
- grapes
- ham
- lettuce
- milk
- onion
- orange
- peas
- peach
- potato
- strawberries
- steak
- tomato

GRAPHIC MASTER 3 - Animal list

ANIMALS

camel	lizard
chicken	ostrich
cow	owl
duck	pig
fish	shark
frog	snake
giraffe	spider
goat	turkey
goldfish	turtle
horse	whale
	zebra

GRAPHIC MASTER 4 - Jobs list

JOBS

artist
barber
bus driver
construction
worker
cook
dentist
doctor
farmer
firefighter
grocer
mail carrier
nurse
pilot
police officer
teacher

GRAPHIC MASTER 5 - Vehicles list

VEHICLES

airplane	motorboat
ambulance	motorcycle
bicycle	pickup truck
boat	police car
bus	school bus
car	ship
fire truck	tractor
helicopter	train

GRAPHIC MASTER 6 - Buildings list

BUILDINGS

- apartment building
- barber shop
- barn
- farm
- fire station
- garage
- gas station
- hospital
- house
- library
- mobile home
- playground
- police station
- post office
- restaurant
- school
- supermarket

GRAPHIC MASTER 7 - How Alike graphic
Use to show how two family members, foods, animals, occupations, vehicles, or buildings are alike.

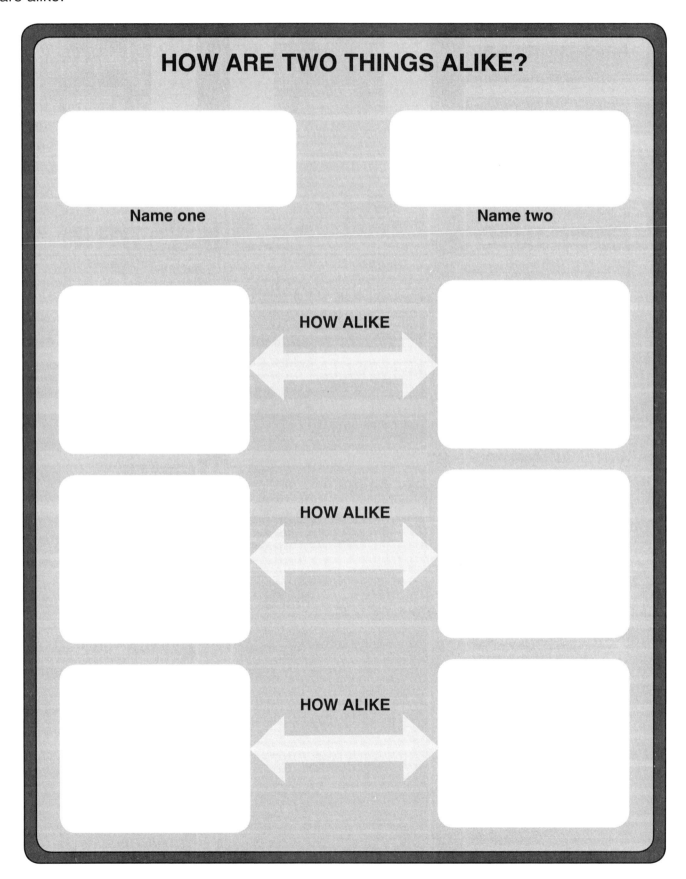

GRAPHIC MASTER 8 - Branching diagram
Use to sort a group into two classes.

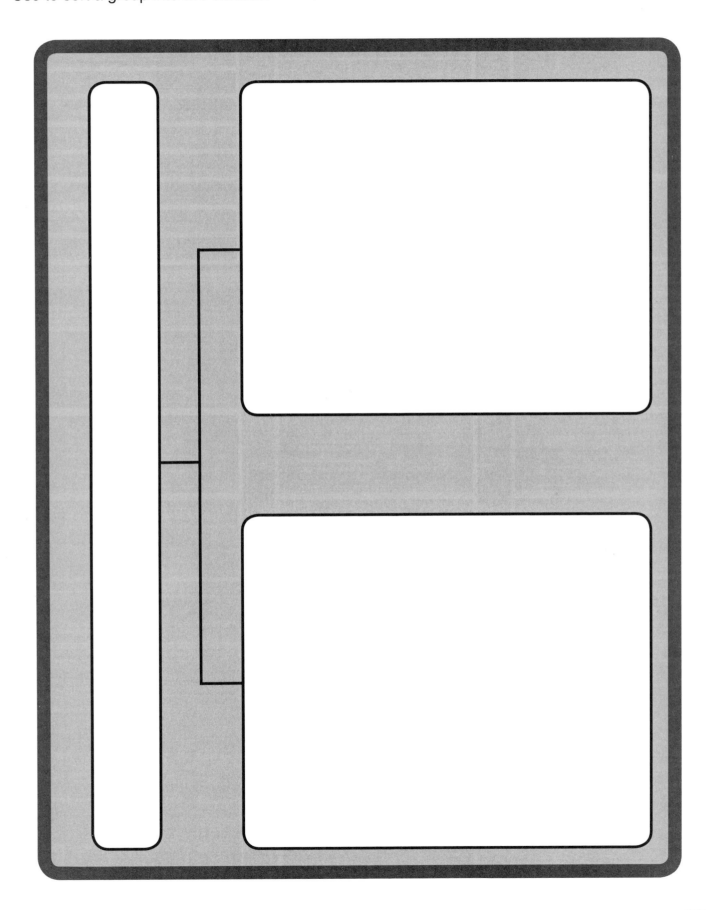

GRAPHIC MASTER 9 - Branching diagram
Use to sort a group into three classes.

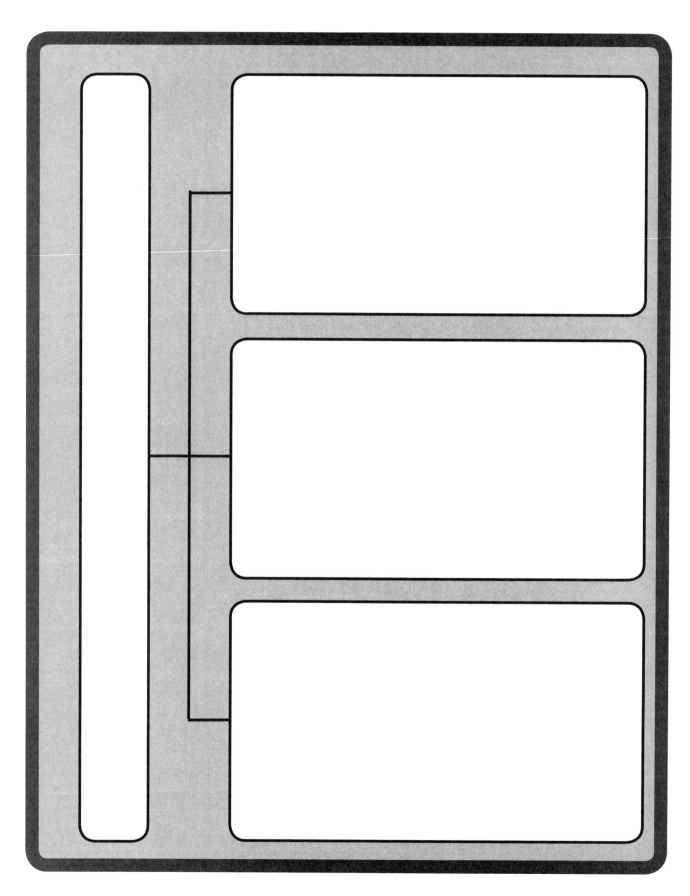

Kindergarten Thinking Skills & Key Concepts — Appendix

GRAPHIC MASTER 10 - Branching diagram
Use to sort a group into four classes.

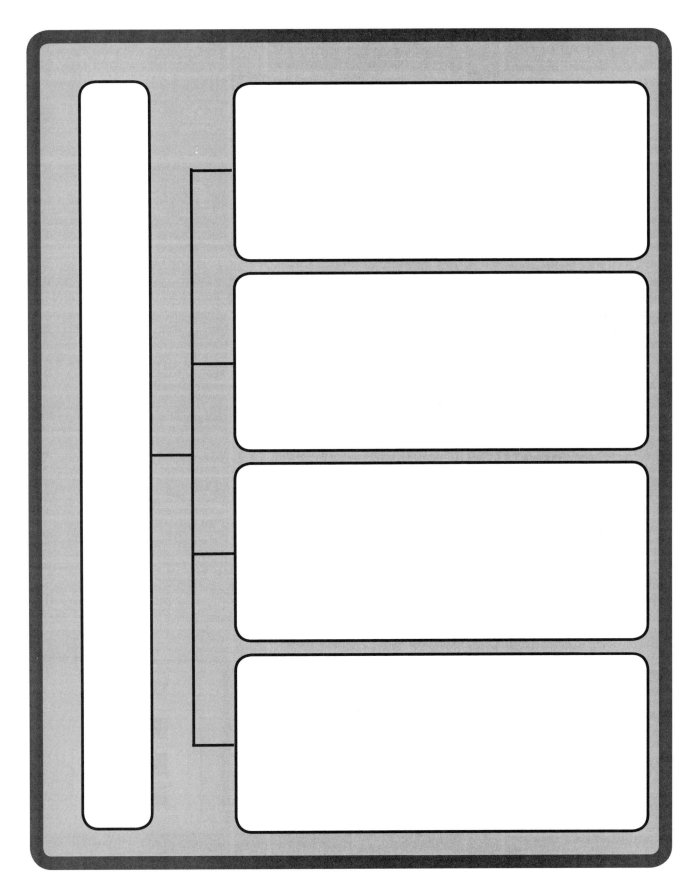

GRAPHIC MASTER 11 - Branching diagram
Use to sort a group into five classes.

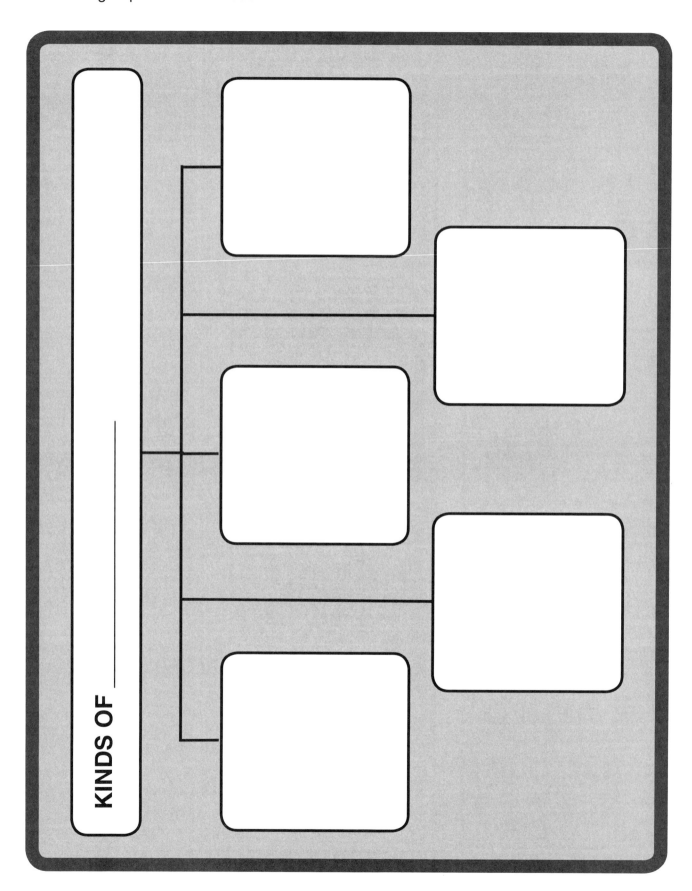